What About Christmas?

Dora D. Flack

Illustrations by Adell Palmer

A Storybook for December

ISBN: 0-88290-000-5
Horizon Publishers' Catalog and Order Number: 1974

First Printing, 1971
Third Revised Printing, 1989

Printed and distributed
in the United States of America by

& Distributors, Incorporated
P.O. Box 490 Bountiful, Utah 84011-0490

About the Author

Dora D. Flack is a writer, dramatist, vocalist, and lecturer. She has combined these talents in presenting thousands of programs and dramatized musical book reviews to church, civic, club, and school audiences in several of the western states. She often uses original stories and material in these programs.

She wrote *What About Christmas?* because of urging from audiences and friends. From personal experience, first with her six children, and now with 24 grandchildren, she knows well the value of family storytimes and activities. Her varied church assignments with youth and women's groups also have given her insight into their literary and entertainment needs.

Several of the stories included in this book have won prizes in writing contests. Many of her other stories and articles have won prizes in the League of Utah Writers contests as well as National League of American Pen Women contests.

In 1969 she won first place in the Juvenile Book Division of the Utah Arts Council writing contests; in 1973 she took second place in their Biography contest, with later articles also winning awards. Two different years she has been a winner in *The Ensign* contests. In 1982 she was named Writer of the Year by the League of Utah Writers. Her articles and stories have been published in many national and church magazines.

Fifteen books which she has written or co-authored have been published, beginning with the best-selling wholewheat cookbook *Wheat for Man*, first published in 1952. Several of her books have been in the foods field: *Fun with Fruit Preservation, Dry and Save* (chosen for a special USA exhibit at the 1978 International Book Fair in Egypt) and *Bread Baking Made Easy.* Biography, how-to and historical books have also been among her publications.

Her short biography appears currently in 20 Who's Who publications: *Who's Who of American Women* and *International Who's Who of Intellectuals*, and others.

Affectionately dedicated
to my patient husband LeGrand
and our six,
Marc, Lane, Kent, Marlane, Karen and Marie,
who know and love the real meaning of
Christmas.

Table of Contents

Preface

For everyone, from earliest youth to the time when eyes grow dim with age, Christmas is a magical time of the year. Cold hearts are warmed by small acts of kindness. Eyes of young and old grow bright, anticipating traditions which are repeated Christmas after Christmas.

A backward glance over the centuries gives us an understanding of the cultures and customs from many lands which have become a part of our present-day Christmas celebrations. Included within these pages are legends, history and stories of Christmas. Some of these stories are fanciful, some are true, and some are true-to-life, written to appeal to varying age groups of a family. Through the pages of this book, may you learn to "keep Christmas" all year; for Christmas and its symbols speak to us of service.

ST. LUKE 2
CHAPTER 2
ST. LUKE 2
A. Palmer

From the Bible we read the account of the first Christmas:

And it came to pass in those days, that there went out a decree from Caesar Augustus, that all the world should be taxed. (And this taxing was first made when Cyreneus was governor of Syria.)

And all went to be taxed, every one into his own city.

And Joseph also went up from Galilee, out of the city of Nazareth, into Judaea, unto the city of David, which is called Bethlehem: (because he was of the house and lineage of David:) To be taxed with Mary his espoused wife, being great with child.

And so it was, that while they were there, the days were accomplished that she should be delivered.

And she brought forth her firstborn son, and wrapped him in swaddling clothes, and laid him in a manger; because there was no room for them in the inn.

And there were in the same country shepherds abiding in the field, keeping watch over their flock by night.

And lo, the angel of the Lord came upon them, and the glory of the Lord shone round about them: and they were sore afraid.

And the angel said unto them, Fear not: for, behold, I bring you good tidings of great joy, which shall be to all people.

For unto you is born this day in the city of David a Saviour, which is Christ the Lord.

And this shall be a sign unto you; Ye shall find the babe wrapped in swaddling clothes, lying in a manger.

And suddenly there was with the angel a multitude of the heavenly host praising God, and saying,

Glory to God in the highest, and on earth peace, good will toward men.

And it came to pass, as the angels were gone away from them into heaven, the shepherds said one to another, Let us now go even unto Bethlehem, and see this thing which is come to pass, which the Lord hath made known unto us.

And they came with haste, and found Mary, and Joseph, and the babe lying in a manger.

And when they had seen it, they made known abroad the saying which was told them concerning this child.

And all they that heard it wondered at those things which were told them by the shepherds.

But Mary kept all these things, and pondered them in her heart.

And the shepherds returned, glorifying and praising God for all the things that they had heard and seen, as it was told unto them.

(Luke 2:1-20)

Now when Jesus was born in Bethlehem of Judaea in the days of Herod the king, behold, there came wise men from the east to Jerusalem, Saying, Where is he that is born King of the Jews? for we have seen his star in the east, and are come to worship him.

When Herod the king had heard these things, he was troubled, and all Jerusalem with him.

And when he had gathered all the chief priests and scribes of the people together, he demanded of them where Christ should be born.

And they said unto him, In Bethlehem of Judaea; for thus it is written by the prophet.

And thou Bethlehem in the land of Juda, art not the least among the princes of Juda: for out of thee shall come a Governor, that shall rule my people Israel.

Then Herod, when he had privily called the wise men, inquired of them diligently what time the star appeared.

And he sent them to Bethlehem, and said, Go and search diligently for the young child; and when ye have found him, bring me word again, that I may come and worship him also.

When they had heard the king, they departed; and, lo, the star, which they saw in the east, went before them, till it came and stood over where the young child was.

When they saw the star they rejoiced with exceeding great joy.

And when they were come into the house, they saw the young child with Mary his mother, and fell down, and worshipped him: and when they had opened their treasures, they presented unto him gifts, gold, and frankincense, and myrrh.

And being warned of God in a dream that they should not return to Herod, they departed into their own country another way.

And when they were departed, behold, the angel of the Lord appeareth to Joseph in a dream, saying, Arise, and take the young child and his mother and flee into Egypt, and be thou there until I bring thee word: for Herod will seek the young child to destroy him.

When he arose, he took the young child and his mother by night, and departed into Egypt:

And was there until the death of Herod: that it might be fulfilled which was spoken of the Lord by the prophet, saying, Out of Egypt have I called my son...

But when Herod was dead, behold, an angel of the Lord appeareth in a dream to Joseph in Egypt, Saying, Arise, and take the young child and his mother, and go into the land of Israel: for they are dead which sought the young child's life.

And he arose, and took the young child and his mother, and came into the land of Israel.

But when he heard that Archelaus did reign in Judaea in the room of his father Herod, he was afraid to go thither: Notwithstanding, being warned of God in a dream, he turned aside into the parts of Galilee:

And he came and dwelt in a city called Nazareth; that it might be fulfilled which was spoken by the prophets, He shall be called a Nazarene.

(Matt. 2:1-23)

Re-reading the account of Christ's birth in the Bible is an important and traditional part of celebrating Christmas. And yet the symbols and traditions of this season go back even before His birth.

From earliest times, many people celebrated the Winter solstice—the season when the days would begin to lengthen. This brought new hope for another year's planting and harvesting. Festivals and feasts were held at that time of the year. We know the month as December.

The early followers of Jesus did not celebrate his birthday. Several hundreds of years passed before the "Christian church" began the observance. Since no one really knew the exact day he was born, it was natural to choose the time of an important festival. December 25th was chosen as the date.

However, the Bible account tells us that the shepherds were watching their flocks in the fields that memorable night. Shepherds took their flocks to the fields in early spring, about the time of Passover, and brought them in again when the first rains came, usually in October. They remained sheltered during the cold winter months. This leads us to believe that the Savior was born in a warm season, probably the spring.

Regardless of the disagreements about the actual date, December 25th—Christmas Day—has become the high spot on the calendar. Christmas is a part of our culture, a time to strengthen ties with family and friends, to turn our thoughts toward the principles the Savior taught. Therefore, many of the Christmas symbols carry a Christian meaning as we celebrate the holiday.

For example:

What About Bells?

The Bible records that bells were used by the Hebrews in their worship in the Tabernacle, being attached to the robe of the priest as he entered the sanctuary. Later they were used around the necks of animals so the master would know of the beast's whereabouts.

Bells have been used in many ancient cultures as a part of their worship. Even the natives in the jungle used their versions of bells to frighten away evil spirits. However, bells were not used in Europe until after the time of Christ. Since then, from the church belfries, bells have called people to worship. They tolled sad death marches. They pealed merrily for a wedding. They sounded an alarm for fires. They rang violently to drive away the thunder and lightning during a storm. They beckoned ships to a safe harbor. They called the people to prayer.

In early Christian times the monks cast and made the bells. Most bellfoundries were located near the abbeys. Centuries later, however, as bells became more popular, large bellfoundries were built in other areas. These factories were owned by families who handed them down for generations from father to son. Perhaps the most famous of all bellfounders were the brothers Frans and Pieter Hemony who lived in the 1600's. The secrets of tuning the bells were guarded carefully by the families.

Bells are made of bronze, which is a mixture of copper and tin. The relative amounts of the two metals are changed to suit the size and tonal need for the bells.

As skill with bell-playing increased, combinations of many bells were used and large carillons[1] *were built and housed in beautiful church towers. Folk songs were kept alive through these carillons, for they can play complicated music. This beautiful bell music is a part of European culture. Belgium is especially famous for its carillons.*

Church bells were often baptized and named, so they could be identified. This was important during World War II, because the Germans took most of the bells made since 1750 and melted them down for machines of war. Only a few were returned to their steeples after the war.

The clangor of bells in Europe is an important part of Christmas. It remains as sweet memories to those who have found homes where the tradition of the bells is not a part of the customs.

---

[1]Pronounced CARE-ih-lahns

Belgian Bells

Paul pulled hard on the rope of the heavy bell. Its clapper moved back and forth against the rim, resounding with a deep, bass peal. Then he pulled the rope of *Jennifer*, the smallest bell in the very top of the belfry. "It sounds as if the tone comes from heaven itself," he thought as he looked up intently and watched the tiny bell swinging and tinkling. He handed the ropes back to the white-haired bellringer. "Merci,[1] Old Jean,[2] for letting me ring the bells." His face was alight from the thrill. "Some day—some day—I'll play a great carillon—" but his voice seemed to float away with the tones of the bells.

Paul raced to the little Belgian cottage he shared with Grandmère.[3] From a distance he could distinguish her outline on the step. He knew her eyes were still closed, lost in the resonance of the fading tones. "Grandmère! Grandmère!" he shouted. "I rang the bells tonight!"

"Did you now?" she smiled. "I thought the sound was not quite as smooth as usual." The light in Paul's eyes vanished, but Grandmère's eyes twinkled mischievously, as she gave him a quick hug. "It was beautiful, but you mustn't get a swelled head. Your playing will improve with practice and age. Morning and night those bells give me the strength for another day, the strength to go on until you are old enough to care for yourself. Then I can close these tired, old eyes forever."

"Grandmère, don't talk like that. You must live until I am a famous carilloneur.[4] I've been watching Old Jean ring his six bells in the parish church. Some day I shall play many, many tunes on many bells—not the same thing over and over."

"Ah-ah, my Paul. Old Jean does his best. You, too, must learn little by little. Our bells are different from any other bells in the world." Very softly in the distance Paul could hear heavenly sounds carried on the wind.

"Do you hear it, Grandmère?" He cocked his head to one side, listening intently.

"Non, my Paul. My old ears can't pick it up any more. Do you hear the carillon from St. Rombaut's[5] cathedral in Mechlin?"

"Hush!" He held up his hand so he wouldn't miss a single tone. The last sounds died away, and Paul sighed. "Grandmère, I must go to Mechlin. I must

---

[1] Pronounced MEHR-see, meaning thank you
[2] Pronounced Zhahn
[3] Pronounced GRAH-mehr, meaning grandmother
[4] Pronounced CAIR-ih-lahn-uhr
[5] Pronounced Saint RAHM-boh

see them, not just hear them on the wind."

"Oui, oui.[6] Tomorrow you may go. You are old enough now to walk there alone. Go and hear. It's in your blood. Your Grandpère[7] rang the bells here most of his life. He, too, wanted to play a carillon." She paused, then went on, "I have not touched the money your parents left. Some day it will pay for you to study with the great Jef Denyn[8] at the carillon school in Mechlin. He's the finest carilloneur. Work hard, my Paul; help me with the crops and grow strong. Who knows what may be ahead of you?"

The next day, Paul didn't even know how he got to the door of St. Rombaut's cathedral in Mechlin. He was so busy listening to the music, he hadn't noticed the bumpy cobblestones. His head was in the clouds, dreaming of the beautiful music he would some day make. At the church door, he looked straight up to the bell tower, rising in majestic stone columns to the very clouds. They were three hundred feet, he'd been told. He admired the ornamentation on the face of the columns and thought they looked like the fine Mechlin lace Grandmère treasured. The stone was darkened from centuries of wind and weather. Reverently he tiptoed into the awesome cathedral and sat down, admiring the arches and paintings.

The church was empty, but at the far end he saw an open door. Could that be the door to the clavier?[9] Almost not daring to breathe, he tiptoed down the aisle toward the door. He peeked inside cautiously and caught his breath. A middle-aged man sat on the padded leather seat in front of the clavier, looking up thoughtfully at wires extending from the dampers and pedals. His hair was well trimmed, white, and stubby on top like white bristles of a brush. He wore a trim goatee which gave a strange, almost humorous appearance to the lined face. The room was almost papered with pictures of men and of other bell towers. Perhaps these were men who had played the carillon in bygone years. Some day would his picture be there? He was so absorbed in examining the room that he forgot he was an intruder. As he took a step, the boards creaked under his foot.

The man almost jumped off the bench. "Who's there?" he snapped. Paul was terrified. He stood rooted in his tracks. The man turned full face toward him. His sharp eyes seemed to penetrate Paul and then they relaxed into a smile behind his gold-rimmed glasses.

"Sneaking in on me to learn my secrets, eh?" The man raised his finger at Paul in mock scolding. "Come, sit here beside me on the bench." Paul's mouth was as dry as chalk. His feet wouldn't move. "Come, don't be afraid. I won't eat you. I'm a carilloneur, not an ogre." A laugh rumbled upward from his ample middle and he slapped his thigh. He slid from the bench and lifted Paul bodily onto it. Paul was bewildered at the many wires, pedals and dampers spread before him.

---

[6] Pronounced wee, wee, meaning "yes, yes"

[7] Pronounced GRAHN-pehr, meaning grandfather

[8] Pronounced Zhef Duh-NEEN

[9] Pronounced KLAH-vee-a

"How—?" But nothing more came out.

"It takes training, my boy—lots of it." Paul's eyes were wide in wonder and curiosity. "Thinking of being a carilloneur some day, my boy?" The man's face was kindly, and his eyes twinkled like Père Noël's.[10]

"I dream of it all the time, Monsieur.[11] Are you Jef Denyn?"

"Indeed I am."

"Will you—will you teach me? See, my legs will reach the pedals now." Paul reached until he almost stood on the pedals.

"But what are you sitting on?" Monsieur Denyn stifled a chuckle, for Paul teetered on the very edge of the bench, his toes barely touching the pedals.

"I'll grow fast, Monsieur, really I will."

"But you must also be very strong. And while you're growing, you keep on ringing the bells at home." Paul relaxed on the bench and leaned against the backrail. Here he was, sitting at the clavier of one of the world's largest carillons—beside the greatest carilloneur in the whole world. And he was treating Paul as a friend, of all things!

"Look straight up, my boy." Monsieur Denyn pointed.

Paul looked up to the rows and rows of bells of different sizes. "There are forty-four bells now. But some day we'll have even more. I've made many changes and additions since I took over from my father, Adolf Denyn. Gradually Father's eyesight faded until I had to take over on Christmas Day of 1887 to do the Christmas concert. He had been the carilloneur since 1849. Since then, I've built up this carillon to be the best there is, with more changes ahead. That's what I was thinking about when you surprised me." He patted Paul's shoulder. "I've given carillon concerts most evenings for a long time until the concerts are part of Mechlin." He glanced at his pocket watch. "It's almost time. By the way, how did you get here?"

"I walked."

"How far?"

"Oh—a few miles," Paul gulped, realizing how tired his legs were; and he was afraid to walk home that far in the dark.

"Where will you stay tonight?"

Paul shrugged his shoulders. "Then you will stay with me in the school. We always have extra beds."

"Oh, merci, Monsieur. But about the bells—"

"Ah, yes. You know, all the bells have been baptized and given names. These were made by thirteen different bellfounders, the best ones, too. See that largest bell? Its name is *Salvator* and it weighs over 17,000 pounds."

"Whew!" Paul let out his breath.

The sounds of many shuffling feet on the stone floor of the cathedral told Monsieur Denyn that his audience had gathered for the evening concert. "You sit on that stool while I play," he smiled.

---

[10] Father Christmas

[11] Pronounced Muh-SYUR, meaning Mr. or Sir

Salvator bonged the hour with deep, bass tones. Paul watched Monsieur Denyn's hands and feet as he worked the pedals and dampers. The chills ran up and down his spine. At times the music would fade to a soft whisper and it reminded Paul of the daintiest pastel on a painting. It was far, far above the tower, like the humming of angels. Then he could hear runs and trills up and down. The sound grew in volume and power until he felt the earth would open and swallow the whole cathedral. Then it faded to light, gay music; he recognized folk tunes. The music held the audience in its spell and they sat in hushed silence, fearing that a whisper would make the music vanish. Paul had never heard anything like it. Inside he felt such a swelling that his body could not contain it—surely he would burst. The goosebumps kept coming and going all over his body. Tears ran down his cheeks, and he shuddered with the thrill. Some day—some day—

At home Paul never forgot the thrill of that memorable night. After school, he labored hard to bring in the harvest. The months slipped away into years. On the front door, occasionally Paul measured his legs, hoping they would grow faster. Physical labor developed his muscles. Running to the bell tower night and morning strengthened his legs. Since listening to the great carillon, he could almost hear some of those sounds above the ringing of the six bells in the village belfry. Often he pulled the bellropes to relieve Old Jean in the tower. Would he ever get to Mechlin again?

The cold winter weather blew in and chilled the villagers. Then sickness swept in. Most of the townspeople stayed behind closed doors because of the dread disease. Grandmère seldom crept out of the warmth of her bed, and she seemed to grow thinner and more pale each day. Paul prepared their meals and waited on her, but she became weaker and weaker. One morning not long before Christmas, Paul ran, as usual, to the church. He climbed the steep steps to the tower. But Old Jean was not there. He peered into the morning haze. Old Jean had never missed a day. Not a living soul was anywhere in sight. It was time for the bells to ring. Grandmère had always said it gave her the strength for another day. He knew others in the village shared her feelings. He grasped the ropes and began to pull. The bells swayed back and forth. But the clapper in the tiny bell, *Jennifer*, was stuck. It wouldn't move. He missed the high, tinkling resonance which gave color when it blended with the deep, somber tone of the bigger bells. He pulled again and again on the small rope, but the bell remained silent.

When the bells quieted, he ran to Old Jean's cottage. He pounded on the door and listened, but heard nothing. He turned the knob and peered in. From the bedroom a faint voice quavered, "Paul?" He found Old Jean huddled under many quilts and knew that he, too, had been stricken.

"Bless you, Paul. The people need the bells, and I couldn't get out of bed. You must go again at noon today and ring them harder to send the sickness away. But why didn't you ring *Jennifer*?"

"I tried, but nothing happened," Paul explained.

"Only *Jennifer* will carry the sickness away into the skies with her delicate tones. They reach heaven best." The old man smiled weakly.

In his heart, Paul knew this was a simple superstition. But perhaps it had such an effect on people that they would try to prove the superstition right, and they would get well from sheer will power. Yes, he must find the way to make *Jennifer* ring.

At home Grandmère asked the same question. "Why didn't you ring *Jennifer*?"

"She's stuck."

"Then unstick her."

"I'll try." He hesitated, then cleared his throat. "Grandmère—I've waited these five long years to hear Monsieur Denyn's Christmas concert. How can I bear to wait another year? The longing eats away at me, but I can't leave you when you're sick."

"Make *Jennifer* ring, and the sickness will leave." She frowned, and the lines in her forehead deepened. "My Paul, you are now big enough and strong enough to go to the carillon school at Mechlin."

"But who will take care of you, Grandmère? I can't leave you alone."

Each day Paul faithfully rang the bells, every hour, but still he couldn't unloose *Jennifer's* tongue. The sickness remained like a dark cloud over the village. Paul knew the bellringer and Grandmère were praying that he wouldn't become ill, too.

The day before Christmas Paul dragged himself up the steep steps to the tower. His head buzzed and ached. He was weak in every joint. In the tower he broke into a cold sweat. He hadn't yet succeeded in getting *Jennifer's* tongue loosened. He grasped a little ball in his pocket, and prayed for strength. Looking down over the village made him dizzy. He grabbed the rope of the big bell. Boom-boom-boom! Then he let go. He took the ball out of his pocket and fixed his gaze on *Jennifer.* "Help me, God, please, help me. The people are depending on me." He drew his arm back and mustering all his strength, he threw the ball straight up. Miraculously the ball reached and tipped *Jennifer's* clapper, and it dropped into position. He grabbed for the rope and pulled frantically. Ding-dong-dong-ding, the tiny bell tinkled joyously. Strength seemed to surge through his body.

"I've done it! I've done it!" he shouted. He pulled all the bellropes in fast succession, which resulted in such a clangor, it could have jolted the sick ones out of their beds. His hair blew in the wind, but Paul tugged on the ropes. At last he let the big bells die away into silence and then, soft and clear, he rang only *Jennifer.* The tinkling sound quieted Paul's troubled soul. He wept uncontrollably as if all the ills of his body were being released through his fingertips into the bellropes and into the bell at the top. He hurried down the steps, hanging onto the rail so he wouldn't fall, and ran to Old Jean's door. He pounded on it with both fists. The door squeaked open. Old Jean stood draped in a quilt with rapture lighting his wrinkled face. Tears coursed down his brown cheeks. "You did it! Paul, you did it! But I am not strong enough to ring the bells tonight for Christmas Eve and tomorrow. You will do it?"

"But I—" Paul bit his lip and hesitated. He nodded, turned and walked away.

His shoulders drooped. What did it matter? Perhaps his own strength had been sapped from the illness until he couldn't walk that far anyhow. Now he must wait a whole year longer. Would he never get to Mechlin? He looked up at the darkening sky and pulled his coat closer. The wind was bitter cold.

He opened the cottage door. There was no welcoming call from Grandmère. The clouds outside made the house seem darker and colder. He stepped to her bedroom door and tapped gently. "Grandmère?" No sound. She must be sleeping. He turned the knob carefully so he wouldn't awaken her and went in. He looked down at the dear, wrinkled sleeping face. A flood of love swept over him. Suddenly he realized all the years of devotion she had given to him, her grandson. Without her, what would have happened to him at the death of his parents? How could he think of leaving her the day before Christmas to walk to Mechlin to hear the concert? Yes, there would be another year. And he must ring the bells for Old Jean. His eyes moved around the room. It had never changed since he could remember. Then his eyes fell upon two heavy cloth bags lying on the lamp table. What were they? He picked them up. Why! They were heavy, and whatever was inside made a dull, clinking noise. He glanced nervously at Grandmère. She was a light sleeper, but she didn't stir. He bent over her. Instinctively he reached out and stroked her forehead. It was cool to his touch. "Grandmère! Grandmère!" he shouted. He sank to his knees beside her bed, as realization dawned on him. Burying his face in the bedcovers, he wept.

At last he gained control of his emotions. He reached up for the bags on the table and opened the drawstrings. Gold coins spilled out onto the floor. What did it mean? Then he recalled Grandmère's words so long ago before he went to Mechlin that memorable day. This was the money Grandmère had saved, his inheritance. He looked at the still face. It was almost as if she had said, "Now you are free to go—go to school and be the carilloneur your Grandpère wanted to be."

As Paul rang the bells that Christmas Eve, all his sorrow and longing and hopes were poured through the bells. Never had they rung so beautifully. They sounded the same—yet different.

Now the bells were silent and he hurried home. Why hurry? What was there without Grandmère? He opened the rough cottage door to go in. Something caught his ear. He pulled the door shut again and turned his head. The impending storm had passed and stars twinkled in a clear sky. Only a gentle breeze played through his hair. That heavenly sound! It was the resonant tones of the Christmas concert at St. Rombaut's, carried to him on the wind. He listened quietly, scarcely breathing. As the last sounds died away, he stared at the closed door. He squared his shoulders and measured his long legs against the mark he had placed on the door long ago. He smiled to himself. Yes, one door had closed behind him, but another was beckoning him to Mechlin. He would stay to play the Christmas bells for Old Jean. And some day—yes, surely—he would play a Christmas concert at Mechlin.

What About Christmas Trees?

When you gaze at a sparkling tree, twinkling with colored lights and ornaments, have you wondered where the custom began?

In the Middle Ages at the Feast Day of Adam and Eve, which was observed December 24th, plays were presented. Among the "props" for the plays was an evergreen tree decorated with apples to remind the audience of the Fall of Adam. Over the years, these folk dramas lost their religious meaning and became crude. So they were outlawed by the church. But the German peasants brought evergreen trees into their homes and decorated them with apples. Later thin cookies were added to remind the people of the "sweets of Redemption." Candles were also used, significant of the "Light of the world." Many years later, the Germans began to make blown-glass baubles, which took the place of the apples on the trees.

From the pages of the past come many legends of Christmas trees and their meaning.

The story is told of St. Boniface, earlier known as Wynfred, who was speaking to a group of his Christian converts on Christmas Eve. When he returned to visit them, he was shocked to find that they had forgotten his teachings of the Christ's sacrifice on the cross for mankind. Instead they were ready to go back to their ancient heathen practices of sacrifice. Thinking to teach them a lesson they would never forget, he cut down a giant oak tree, which was one of the symbols of worship of the Druids. As it fell to the earth, it split into four pieces. He indicated a young fir tree growing nearby, pointing a green spire toward the sky. Boniface pointed to the tree and said to his followers: "This young child of the forest, this tree, shall be your holy tree tonight. Your houses are built of the Fir, so it is the wood of peace. Its leaves are evergreen, so it is the sign of everlasting life. See how it points toward the heaven. Let this tree turn your thoughts upward. Gather about such a tree in your own homes. There it shall be surrounded with loving gifts and rites of kindness."

From France comes the tale of Bonchevalier[1] *who lived many, many years ago. It was Christmas Eve, and he was traveling on horseback through the deep forest. Suddenly in the distance, he saw a tall evergreen tree. He blinked his eyes and looked harder, for the tree glowed with lights, and a bright star seemed to rest in the topmost branches. As he drew closer, he was amazed to see that the tree was covered with candles. Strangely some of the candles hung down and others stood upright. In the light of the star at the top of the tree, he saw the vision of a child with a bright light around his head. The story goes on to say that he told this experience to the wise men in his community. But they only shook their heads, not being able to tell him what it meant. When he told his mother, she nodded and said, "Your journey through the dark forest has revealed to you the Tree of Humanity. The candles were people. The good persons were represented by the upright candles. The bad ones were hanging down. The child at the top, of course, is the Infant Jesus who watches over the world of humanity."*

---

[1] Pronounced Bohn-she-VAHL-ya

Another tale is told of Martin Luther. He was born in 1483 in Germany. Luther loved the story of the Nativity. One Christmas Eve he wandered out into the cold and snow to meditate on the wonder of the birth of the Savior. In Germany in December the snow covers everything with a deep blanket of white. The days are short and the nights are long, and it is bitter cold.

On this Christmas Eve Luther, bundled in his warmest clothes, walked the countryside, gazing into the clear, star-studded sky. The stars appeared to be jewels overhead. He looked at the white-covered evergreens, weighted down with the snow, which seemed to be covered with jewels also. He cut a small fir tree and took it home. Then he set it up in his house and fastened lighted candles to the branches, reminding him of the lights in the sky. His children were delighted with the tree. Whether this is fact or legend is not known, but he is generally given credit for the first lighted Christmas tree indoors.

The Christmas tree was transplanted from Germany to England. Queen Victoria married Prince Albert from Saxe-Coburg, Germany. The year after their first son was born in 1848, Prince Albert had an evergreen tree decorated, and he introduced the custom to England. The **Illustrated London News** *carried a detailed story and picture of this tree. Of course, settlers had previously come from Germany to England and they had brought the tradition of the Christmas Tree with them. But now that it had found its way into the palace of the Queen, the custom grew and spread.*

When the Puritans first came to America, their religious beliefs frowned upon the celebration of Christmas. Some of the men refused to work on Christmas Day. So in December of 1621, Governor Bradford of the Plymouth colony stated that "if they made it a matter of conscience, he would spare them till they were better informed." However, it is important to note that their celebrating was anything but religious, but was "revelling, dicing, carding, masking, mumming."

In May, 1659 in the Plymouth colony, a law was passed which forbade observing Christmas in any way. Five shillings was set as the fine. The law was repealed in 1689.

German immigrants brought the custom of the Christmas tree with them to America. The tradition spread throughout the United States.

Like Christmas music, the Christmas tree has been almost a universal language in Christian nations. The **New York Times** *carried an interesting account of an incident during World War I in 1914. It was Christmas Eve and suddenly gray-uniformed figures from the German trenches came over to the English soldiers in the front lines of France, carrying little Christmas trees. They cried in broken English, "Merry Christmas, Tommy!" That Christmas Eve, lighted Christmas trees formed a chain of lights from the front lines in France to German headquarters. Suddenly men from both sides were scrambling into No-Man's-Land, laughing, cheering and singing. Rifles were laid aside and hands were clasped in friendship. The German soldiers sang* **Stille Nacht, Heilige Nacht** *(Silent Night, Holy Night) and* **O Tannenbaum,** *and the English responded with* **Good King Wenceslas.**

Who can tell the bitter feelings that have been buried beside a lighted Christmas tree and the "good will toward men" which has taken their place?

The Legend of the Foolish Fir Tree

On a snow-covered mountainside grew a little Fir Tree. Although she was still a young tree, she stood tall and straight and her pointed tip reached for the sky. Surrounding her were other trees of great beauty: shapely maples, shimmering aspens, and giant evergreens. In the spring the gray branches of the leafy trees were covered with tiny buds. Their buds swelled and burst into fresh, new green leaves which grew until the limbs were completely covered. The leaves fluttered and swayed in the breeze. The Fir Tree saw that they were graceful trees, and she envied their beautiful, soft dresses. As summer faded into autumn, the Fir Tree watched the green on the other trees change to yellow, bronze, and scarlet. The mountainside seemed to be ablaze with the breath-taking color. Then she *was* envious as she looked at her stiff, green needles which never changed with the seasons. Her drab dress always looked the same.

"Oh, why must I have such an ugly, old dress?" the Fir Tree cried. "No one notices me. Even when I've grown up I'll still look the same. I'm tired of this old garb. If the fairies of the forest would ask me, I'd tell them in a hurry how I'd like to be dressed. Why, I'd like to have leaves of gold, and then everyone would notice me."

The Fir Tree fretted and stewed about her dress until night fell and blotted out the colored leaves of the other trees. Then she fell asleep. During the night, cold frost crept through the forest. The wind raced in swirls and gales, swishing through branches, and the Fir Tree shivered in her sleep. When she awoke in the dull gray of the morning, she looked around at her brilliant companions. The ground was strewn with scarlet, yellow, and brown leaves. The trees around her looked less gay, for their dresses had become thin and ragged.

Then she looked down at her own branches and blinked her eyes. In place of the stiff, green needles, her limbs were covered with leaves of solid gold. "I knew it," she beamed. "I knew all I had to do was to tell the fairies how ugly I was and they would grant my wish." Then she puffed herself up very straight and tall and knew her dress was the fairest of all. "Why, not one of the trees is as pretty as I am, I guess." As the sun came out from behind the clouds, she preened and she beamed in the sun until the other trees wanted to move right away from her, but, of course, they couldn't.

The sun shone brightly and played on every shining leaf of gold so that the Fir Tree, in spite of her small size, stood out from all the other trees in splendor. Just then a peddler passed that way and he stopped dead in his tracks. "A gold tree?" he mused. "Can't be." So he walked up and touched the golden leaves with care. "Bless my soul! It's real. This will make me rich." He opened his pack and carefully plucked the golden leaves until he could hardly lift his pack to his shoulder. With a wide grin on his face, he turned and walked away and left the Fir Tree bare.

The Fir Tree shivered as the night breezes blew. "How foolish I was to wish for golden leaves," she said. "I should have known humans would want my gold. If the fairies would hear me again, I'd wish for something that would cost much less." She thought and she thought and then brightened as an idea struck her. "I wish—I wish for glass for my dress." In spite of the cold, she finally fell asleep. The fairies laughed as they danced around the Fir Tree that night, but they granted her second wish.

At last the cold night was past, and the sun warmed her with its cheering rays. When she looked down at her dress, she was almost blinded by the sparkling leaves of glass on every branch. The sun's rays danced on the glass leaves and made the tree look like a huge, crystal chandelier.

"I knew it!" she beamed. "I knew glass would make a dazzling dress. No one would ever steal glass leaves. Why, not one of the trees is as pretty as I am, I guess." She preened and she beamed in the sun and boasted to the other trees until they wanted to move right away from her, but of course they couldn't.

The day drew on and the Fir Tree grew more boastful. Suddenly, a rude wind had heard as much as he could bear, and he dashed through the forest in a temper. The wind shook the glass leaves together and they broke into millions of pieces and fell to the ground, with a smashing, tinkling sound. The wind raced back and forth creating a real stir and the tree was chilled to the sap. She moaned, "Oh, why didn't I remember that glass would break! How foolish I've been. I know it's asking a lot, but if the fairies would hear me again, this time I wouldn't make a mistake." She thought and she thought and then brightened as an idea struck her.

"If the fairies would only hear me again, it wouldn't cost much to grant my wish. In leaves of green lettuce, I'd choose to be dressed." At last the Fir Tree fell asleep.

The fairies came once again and danced around the tree, but it was hard to dance because they were laughing so hard. Their magic wands lightly touched each branch of the Tree. Then they skittered away. When the sun rose in the morning, the Fir Tree could still hear their tinkling laughter. But when she looked at her branches, she was the happiest tree in the forest. She was covered from tip to toe with juicy leaves of green lettuce. The wind stirred the ruffled edges of each leaf and she said, "I knew it. None of the trees is as pretty as I am, I guess." And she preened and she beamed in the sun and boasted to the other trees until they wanted to move right away from her, but of course they couldn't.

A shaggy goat was out for an afternoon walk and overheard the Fir Tree's talk. He pricked up his ears and walked nearer to the tree. His mouth began to water and he said, "I agree. You're the prettiest tree in the whole forest. I want your leaves for my five o'clock tea." Without stopping to say grace, he ate every tender, young leaf and walked away with a grin on his face.

The Fir Tree shivered and shook in the evening wind, but she didn't utter a word. She was disgraced. She realized now what a fool she'd been to think she could choose her own dress. Nature didn't work that way. At last night fell and she sank into a deep, deep sleep. All night long nightmares punished her. She knew she'd learned her lesson. She'd have to live forever with bare branches, but she'd be big about it. She'd never complain.

Morning came and the Fir Tree awoke to a world of white. Snow had fallen during the night and covered the forest with a beautiful blanket of white. The sun sparkled on the snow, making it look as if the fairies had thrown handfuls of diamonds everywhere. Bare branches of other trees were glistening. She looked down at her own limbs, hoping they'd be just a bit beautiful with snow to cover them. She blinked and shut her eyes. Then she opened them and blinked again. She must be seeing things. Her branches were covered with straight, sharp, green needles under the snow. In the sun she, too, looked as if she were covered with diamonds.

In the distance she could hear happy human voices. As they waded through the snow, they laughed and sang. One human shouted, "No, not that one. Look over here." He came up to the little Fir Tree and exclaimed with joy, "Here it is! Here's the perfect Christmas tree!"

The Christmas Intruder

"Dad, please help us trim the tree." Joy's arms curved around his neck coaxingly as he sat in the easy chair with head down. "Dad, even if Rick isn't here, he'd want us to enjoy Christmas."

Dad sighed heavily. "Why must we have Christmas at all this year? If they had just flown Rick back from Vietnam, or if they'd told us how seriously he's hurt—"

"Dad, I'm worried about Rick, too. But we have to know they're doing everything they can for him, wherever he is," Joy said.

"She's right," Mother agreed. "If we try to have Christmas as usual, we'll feel better. We can't just give up."

"If we only knew where he is—"

Mother ventured, "You've done an excellent job of barbering this shaggy tree. Even though it's a leftover, it's as trim as your haircuts. Come on, Honey, Joy must have a tree even though we've put it off till Christmas Eve because of our worry."

Dad squared his shoulders and swallowed hard. "Where are the lights, Mother?" From the stack of decorations in boxes, Mother picked out the strings of lights and handed them to him. Without a word, he carefully strung them down the trunk of the tree. Mother sorted the boxes of ornaments to be used, and handed them one by one to Joy, who hung them on the lower branches while Mother worked at the top.

"We have to have the star. That was always Rick's favorite," Joy bubbled. She saw Dad bite his lip. Then he turned and left the room.

Arm in arm Joy and her mother stood staring into the crackling fire in the fireplace. It sent dancing shadows on the walls. From the kitchen came the fragrant odor of spiced cider which would provide a snack, with fresh cookies, to be enjoyed around the fireplace after the tree-trimming. Joy switched on the stereo. Christmas carols filled the air. She stepped to the window and looked out at the giant, lazy snowflakes gentling to the ground. A white Christmas—Rick's yearly wish. Why, it was like a fairyland outside. The world was beautiful, and it was Christmas Eve! This was the best night of the year. Or it would be if Rick could be home. She stared out the window, not really seeing anything. Suddenly her eyes popped into sharp focus. Who was that boy standing on the steps?

"Mother?" she whispered. "Out there—that boy—" As Mother stepped to the window, the boy turned to walk down the porch steps. In a flash, Mother opened the front door. At her invitation, the boy came in. He was shaggy and unkempt, about fourteen years old. His uncombed hair was growing over his ears and hung over his shirt collar. Snow frosted his hair and covered his thin, shabby coat. His shoulders were hunched and his hands were stuffed in his pockets. His face was pinched and blue from cold.

"I couldn't let him stay out in the cold," Mother explained, her hand resting lightly on his shoulder. Into Joy's mind flashed a picture of two strangers at an inn door two thousand years ago. She was glad Mother wasn't like that innkeeper. They had room, but what about Dad? What would he say?

"I'll bet you're hungry," Joy ventured.

Not hearing, the boy stood staring at the tree, the lights reflected in his somber eyes. "Could I help trim it?" he spoke almost in a whisper. "I've been watching from outside. Everyone else has the tree trimmed. I always helped with ours at home." His shoulders relaxed as he spoke, and he held his chilled fingers out to the warmth of the blaze, rubbing them hard.

"Where is home?" Mother asked.

"In Sawyer," he said, hanging his head.

"That's thirty miles from here. Why aren't you there on Christmas Eve?"

The boy cleared his throat and hesitated. "I ran away—a couple of days ago."

"Why?" Joy asked.

"I got mad at my dad. He won't let me grow my hair long. He said, 'Get it cut or get out.' So I got out. What a stupid clod I am. Out there, watching you—in here—I—" He dug his hands into his pockets. In the silence, his stomach growled. He blinked hard.

"Here, take off your coat and wash your hands while Joy fixes you a sandwich. You must be starved," Mother said. Almost before you could say "Merry Christmas!" Joy set a tuna sandwich, chips, and a glass of milk in front of him at the kitchen table.

Joy looked up to see Dad standing in the doorway, his eyes clouded. She knew what he was thinking. He hated long hair with a passion. It not only hurt his barber business, but he could talk long and loud about shaggy hair and revolution against the establishment. She knew he would have turned the boy away. Inside she wondered what it would do to Dad if Rick were like this boy.

"Oh!" Mother looked up, startled to see Dad. "Honey, this is—I didn't even ask your name."

"Boden—Jim Boden," the boy said, as he gulped his milk. It was obvious that he hadn't eaten in quite a while.

"What do you mean, letting a stranger in the house? You never know what they might do or what they might be hiding." Suddenly Dad was red-faced at his own rudeness.

"I'm not hiding anything—honest, Sir," Jim stammered.

"He's cold and hungry and wants to help trim the tree," Mother said quietly. "Jim, wouldn't you like to call your mother on the telephone?"

"I sure would, but I'm broke. And it's long distance. Hey, maybe I could reverse the charges. Do you think Dad would still be too mad at me?"

"Not on Christmas Eve," Mother smiled. "I think they'd be so relieved to know where you are, they'd let you work it out when you got home."

"Yeah, and I'd do it, too. I wonder if Dad would come and get me. I've learned my lesson for sure. But it's too late. The barber shops are closed. Anyhow I haven't got the price of a haircut. How could I be so dumb to think I could earn my own way? Nobody will hire you till you're sixteen. I got sick of always being under Dad's thumb, but I wish I was back there now—I'll bet he needs me in his bakery." As he talked, his eyes shone and his whole face brightened. Joy noticed how shabby his clothes were, but lots of boys who could afford good clothes looked that bad—and worse.

While Jim telephoned his parents, Mother, Dad, and Joy proceeded with the tree-trimming. Joy felt a warm feeling inside. Dad was helping. Was he humming?

Jim hung up the phone. "What's the matter, Jim?" Mother asked.

"They're not coming to get me. The old jitney's got a broken block. No transportation."

"Oh, what a shame," Mother sympathized.

"That's not all. Mom wants me home, but Dad says not until my hair is cut." He picked up a bauble and hung it on the end of a branch. "Wonder where I go from here." He seemed to enjoy the family feeling in spite of his problem.

"Could he stay here, Daddy?" Joy asked excitedly.

"No." Her excitement died on her lips. "A boy should be home—"

"You're right," Jim agreed. "I'm never going to be so stupid again. But I'll be on my way." He reached for his jacket.

"But where will you go?" Joy asked.

"Where have you stayed since you left home?" Mother inquired.

"Oh, I curled up in somebody's garage last night. It was sure cold though. I dunno where I'll go tonight."

"Not so fast, young man," Dad said, his tone light for the first time that evening. "Do you really want to go home?"

"Golly, there's nothin' I'd like better, but I can't. Even if I could hitch a ride home tonight, my hair's still long. I thought I wanted to be like the cool guys, but they just mean trouble. Dad said, long hair and a bakery don't mix. Guess he knows what he's talkin' about when he says I gotta work. He keeps preachin' 'An idle mind is the devil's workshop.' He could be right, 'cause the guys get into a heap o' trouble cruisin' around."

"Well, if you've really learned your lesson, you might find you knocked on the right door tonight," Dad said.

"What do you mean?" Jim was puzzled.

"I'm a barber. We could go down to the shop—"

"No kiddin'? Then I could hitch a ride home and maybe I could be sleepin' in my own bed tonight."

"Tell you what, Jim," Mother interrupted. "Why don't you go in and take a hot bath and wash your hair. Our son's clothes would just about fit you, I believe."

"Wouldn't your mother and dad be glad to see you all slicked up?" Joy grinned. "But what if he can't hitch a ride home, Dad? You always say it's against the law. Couldn't he stay here tonight, so he won't get cold again?"

"No, he can't stay here. We'll drive him home and make sure he gets there. But I don't like to leave the phone."

"I'll stay, in case anyone should call," Joy agreed.

"How can I thank you for not turning me away? This is the greatest Christmas of my life."

"Let's hope it changes your life," Dad said. "I want to meet your dad and let him know how lucky he is—to have a son home. If we only knew about ours—"

The phone jangled. Dad almost tripped in his eagerness to grab it. But Joy answered first.

"Hello," she bubbled. In the breathless silence, they all heard a noise like coins dropping into a pay phone.

Joy handed the phone to Dad as an excited voice said, "Hello! Hello!" It was Rick's voice.

"Are you all right, Son?" Dad asked. Joy was so excited she felt like screaming. Dad held the phone away from his ear.

"Rick's voice is so loud, he doesn't need a phone," Joy giggled.

"Don't worry about me. I'm not badly wounded," Rick shouted. "Have you got the tree trimmed? I'm in 'Frisco. They're flying me out of here in the morning. I'll be home for Christmas dinner!"

What About Lights?

Our Christmas candles come from the ancient Hebrew festival known as Chanukkah, or the **Feast of Lights**. *It happens to fall at the Christmas season and observes the re-dedication of the Temple.*

But the light of a candle reminds Christians of the words of the Savior: I AM THE LIGHT OF THE WORLD. I AM THE RESURRECTION AND THE LIFE. *The light becomes a sermon in itself.*

Finnish Lights

Christmas will never be the same without Mummo,"[1] Raija[2] sighed, as she gazed out the bedroom window at the Finnish landscape.

"Even Mummo couldn't live forever, Raija. But we'll never forget her. I miss her goodness and love, but when I think of her, I get a good, warm feeling inside," Pirkko[3] said.

"If she had only finished dressing the Mummo doll before she died, then I'd always have something of hers. That's what I wanted for Christmas more than anything. Mama promised to finish it—" Raija caught herself.

"But you know she's been far too busy," Pirkko added.

Raija thought gloomily, Pirkko might as well have said it—I'm always thinking only of what I want. That's not like Mummo, so I don't deserve her doll.

"Let's go downstairs and help Mama get dinner on," Pirkko suggested. "It's 2:30 and soon dark. Old Mrs. Virta will be here with her grandchildren before we're ready for them."

"Why did Mama have to invite *them* to spend Christmas Eve with us? We'll have to sing and dance with them around the tree like little kids," Raija complained.

"Mama is like Mummo—always sharing. She knows how hard it is for Mrs. Virta to do a real Christmas dinner for her motherless grandchildren. So at least we can help to entertain them," Pirkko said.

"I've wrapped a present for all three of the children. That's enough," Raija said. Whoops, there it is again. What did Mummo always say? *The gift without the giver is bare.*

Downstairs the two sisters helped arrange the serving table. Mrs. Virta's face glowed to see such a meal and the children's eyes seemed as big as plates. Raija thought they might never have seen so much food. There was:

Herring Salad (made from herring and diced vegetables in a thick, creamy pink sauce).
Cobbler's Sprats (herring filets dipped in vinegar, onion, allspice, sugar, and slices of raw carrots).
Jellied veal and pressed brawn.
Liver paste (for dipping bread).
Baked ham.

---

[1] Pronounced MOO-moh, meaning grandmother
[2] Pronounced RI-yuh
[3] Pronounced PEER-koh

Casseroles (made from rhutabegas, turnips, carrots, potatoes, and liver).
Dried green peas (soaked overnight, then rinsed, seasoned and baked).
Kalja (a non-alcoholic beer made from rye, malt, water, sugar, and yeast).
Lutefisk with white sauce.
Rice (cooked in milk and topped with cinnamon and sugar. An almond is secretly placed in one saucer of rice, but no one knows which dish. The lucky finder can wish on the almond.)

Here was a meal to tickle the palate of any Finn. Every person ate the rice slowly, trying to find the almond, but also keeping it a secret. Raija's spoon hit something hard. Now she ate very slowly to hide the almond, so she wouldn't spoil the surprise for everyone else. My wish? she thought—for the Mummo doll, of course.

Following the dinner there were Christmas carols to be sung and Pa-pa read the Nativity from Luke before going to church for candle-light services. Then, after church, Pa-pa disappeared.

Next the graves in the cemetery must be lighted. While Mrs. Virta and the children returned home for their grave light, Raija collected the equipment for Mummo's grave. Bundled in her warm wool coat and fur cap, she wrapped her elegant blue-and-white wool scarf around her neck. Mummo had made the scarf. It kept her warm and snug on the outside. She put on her knitted mittens and ran to the gate where Pirkko waited with the foot sleigh. Raija jumped in and they were off. The sleigh resembled a chair sitting on flat, metal runners. Pirkko grasped the back of the chair and started off toward the cemetery. One foot rode a runner and the other foot pushed the sleigh forward.

At the top of the hill, she placed both feet squarely on the runners and they sailed down the slick incline. "Whee!" they both laughed. Their cheeks were ruddy from the frosty air whizzing by them. In all directions people were moving toward the cemetery. Some went in cars. But the foot-sleigh was more fun. Raija hung onto the broom, the glass lamp, the candle, and a box of matches.

At Mummo's grave, Raija put the candle in its base. It was about 2 inches in diameter and 4 inches tall, with a heavy wick. Now the trick was to get it lighted with the howling wind ready to snuff out the flame before she could place the chimney over it. She scraped the match on the sandpaper. It flared, but the wind blew it out. "Raija, did you bring the little kitchen matches?" Pirkko groaned.

"Of course," Raija said.

"Don't you know we have to have the special long ones?"

"No! Why do I do everything wrong?" Raija groaned.

Pirkko gave her a glance of disgust. She took off her gloves. Her fingers were stiff with cold. "Now you be ready to protect the flame with your hands." The wick lighted. "Hurry! Get the chimney over it, Raija."

With her mittens on, Raija was all thumbs and she dropped the glass globe. "Thank goodness, it didn't break," she breathed.

Again Pirkko struck the match, but it flickered out. Striking another match and with Raija holding her hands around the elusive flame, it blazed. With blue fingers, Raija slipped the cover carefully over the candle. It burned. Raija held her breath until the flame was steady. Then she stood up and gazed out across the sea of twinkling lights. The scene took her breath away—blocks and blocks of tiny flames—a burning candle on every grave. A great reverence stole over her. What had Mummo said? The lights are to remind us that Jesus is the Light of the world and through Him we shall all live again.

Pirkko broke into her thoughts. "Come, Raija, let's finish the grave and hurry home before our noses are frostbitten."

"Let me do it, Pirkko," Raija said. With the broom she swept out the footsteps around the grave so it would look untouched.

Mrs. Virta and the children were already waiting when the girls arrived home. She was wiping her nose, still chilled from the walk to the cemetery. "My old wool scarf is getting too thin to keep my head warm," Mrs. Virta said. Raija wished she could take away the sad look on Mrs. Virta's face. She slipped out of the room. When she returned, she carried four packages which she dropped in the fancy laundry basket by the front door. The basket was filled with presents waiting for Joulupukki[4] to distribute them. To each package was attached a rhyme which was a clue to the contents.

"Come, Anja,[5] Marja,[6] Matti,"[7] Raija said. "It's time for singing and dancing. They formed a circle around the tree and dramatized and sang the many songs known to all Finnish children. The little children loved having Raija and Pirkko play with them. They all laughed at little Matti's lisping efforts and loved him the more for them. Suddenly a knock was heard at the door. "Joulupukki!" the little ones cried, scurrying to their grandmother. Mama opened the door and there stood Joulupukki dressed in a long wolfskin coat. Raija and Pirkko kept straight faces, for they knew it was Pa-pa who had been out Santa Clausing at other homes and was now back to distribute the gifts in their own basket.

"Have you been a good boy, Matti?" Joulupukki asked in a deep voice.

Raija stifled a giggle because Matti's face was a puzzle-mixture of laughter, excitement, fear, and tears. So Joulupukki picked up a gift from the basket. "Ah-ha, the rhyme reads: 'If you will be good, here's a soldier of wood.'" It was Raija's gift for Matti.

The other gifts were passed out by Joulupukki with mock seriousness. The last present was handed to Mrs. Virta. She read the rhyme:

"Round my neck I wind and wind,
Then I never get cold from behind."

Everyone laughed as Mrs. Virta unwrapped Raija's elegant blue-and-white scarf. "Not this!" she exclaimed. "Your mummo made it for you last year."

"It will keep *you* warm now. Mummo would want it that way. I have my old

---

[4]Pronounced YOH-loo-poo-kee, meaning Santa Claus
[5]Pronounced AHN-yah
[6]Pronounced MAHR-ee-ah
[7]Pronounced MAH-tee

one to wear until I can knit a new one," Raija said.

Then to the children's surprise Joulupukki took off his coat.

Matti was shocked, "Joulupukki—your Pa-pa?" he grinned. Everyone giggled.

But Raija was disappointed. The Mummo doll was not among her gifts. She had expected Mama to perform a miracle and finish it in spite of her rush.

Six o'clock came early next morning and everyone was on the way to church again. Raija and Pirkko were warm under the robes in the big horse-drawn sleigh. Mama held the burning torch high. Of course, pitch-darkness was everywhere around them, except for the flaming torches in each sleigh or wagon. Poor people were on foot. Pa-pa opened the door of the lighted church and Raija caught her breath. Lighted candles made the church a fairyland of flame. Never had she seen anything so splendid. The organ played Christmas carols softly while the worshippers took their places. Much singing was followed by a Christmas message from the minister. Raija couldn't concentrate on the minister's words. She was thinking about the exciting race home with the other horses and sleighs.

At home Mama served hot chocolate and Christmas bread: Lucia's Cats and Priest's Hair. (The Priest's Hair is made with three short strips of dough curled like a wig with a raisin in the end of each curl). Raija was so weary she felt like sleeping at the table. Then she noticed dark circles under her mother's eyes. "Mama, you need a long nap. I'll do the dishes and then when it's dinnertime I'll get it on the table." She felt a warm glow inside. Now she knew what Mummo had meant in her rhyme with the wool scarf last Christmas. In her mind Raija repeated it:

"This gift can warm you on the outside,
Only you can make the warmth inside."

Was this Mummo's secret of happiness? She was always doing for others, never thinking of herself. Raija hadn't deserved the doll—that's why Mama hadn't found time to finish it.

Outside it was still dark. After straightening the kitchen, Raija donned her nightie and slipped in bed beside Pirkko. She felt something on the pillow. What could it be? Her hand felt for the object and she was wide awake. "The light, Pirkko. Quick!" She blinked back happy tears as she hugged the Mummo doll close. "Now I know why Mama is so sleepy. Oh, I don't deserve it."

Pirkko picked up the rhyme on the pillow beside the doll. It read:

"Mummo rejoices that you have learned
The kind ways by which you have earned
The great blessings of Christmas joy,
Which all the year you must employ."

"My almond wish did come true. The doll will always remind me to think of others." Raija snuggled down under the covers with the Mummo doll on the pillow beside her.

A Swedish Lucia

Karin[1] breezed down the stairs and glanced out the window at the deep, swirling snow. The morning paper lay open on the sofa. On the front page she caught a headline: "*Saint Lucia*[2] *Winner To Be Announced Tomorrow.*" Karin sighed. "I can't be Lucia in my own home, much less in the whole town of Boden," she thought to herself. "Why am I so thoughtless?" Suddenly she remembered the condition of her room. She raced upstairs and found Roberta straightening covers on her bed. Karin grabbed the covers on her side.

"Sorry, Roberta, I didn't mean to leave it all for you. Just didn't think," she apologized. The golden-haired girls looked enough alike to be Swedish sisters, even though Roberta was an American Exchange student living with Karin's family for the school year. The girls attended high school together.

"Oh, that's all right," Roberta replied. "You've really improved this last month. Now you do more than your share."

"Saint Lucia for our town will be announced tomorrow and that reminded me that I still have a long way to go."

"What do you mean?" Roberta asked.

"Christmas season is ushered in every year on December 13th with Lucia and our Festival of Lights. One girl in the home is selected as Lucia. It's an honor for only the kindest girl in the family. I've really been trying this year, hoping Mother will choose me just once. But this morning proves that I'm still thoughtless. Well, if I hurry I can beat Anna downstairs to help Mother with breakfast."

"I'll help too and you can tell me more about Lucia. This is fun learning about your customs," Roberta smiled.

"I think you'll like our traditions." While the girls hurried to get breakfast on the table, Karin explained. "Saint Lucia lived in Sicily. She became converted to Christianity but her people hated the Christians. She went about doing so much good that her countrymen hated her too—said she was acting like a Christian. They finally burned her at the stake."

"How awful," Roberta grimaced.

"So centuries ago the Festival of Lights became part of our celebration to remind us to be like her. That's why only the best girl in a family is chosen. Each town chooses a Lucia and she's queen of Christmas. It's every Swedish girl's fondest dream. But I'd never make it."

"Why do you say that?" Roberta asked, placing silverware at each place on the

---

[1]Pronounced CAR-in
[2]Pronounced Loo-SEE-uh

table. "I've noticed how you've gone out of your way at school to help Kristin since she's been on crutches. There were lots of times you were in a hurry. But you never let her know it. When we've done volunteer work at the hospital, the children would rather have you tell stories than anyone else. And that Mrs. Larson! How can you go and read to her and take her complaining?"

The telephone rang and Karin answered it. "Hello ... Yes, Mrs. Larson, this is Karin. ... Well—I planned to stay after school for a club meeting. ..." Karin bit her lip. "All right, Mrs. Larson, I'll come as soon as school is out." She slammed the phone back on the hook. "Ooooh! She makes me furious. She said I should be grateful I can walk. If I knew her pain I'd gladly come and read to get her mind off it! Doesn't she know there are things *I* want to do, too?"

"Here, here, what's all the ranting?" Mother asked.

"I'm sorry, Mother." Karin checked her temper.

"And you who wants to be our family Lucia. By the way, Karin, how about Roberta being Lucia this year? She'll never get another chance."

Karin turned to the sink to get a drink of water so she could hide the tears that wanted to spill over.

"Oh, no," Roberta objected. "Don't you know how much this means to Karin?"

Karin managed a smile. "Perhaps next year I'll deserve to be Lucia. As Mother says, this is your only chance. Hurry—we'll be late for school."

After school Roberta stayed at the gym to play ball with the other girls and Karin plodded through the snow to Mrs. Larson's big house. A servant let her in.

"Come in, Karin," Mrs. Larson called. Karin entered the living room where the elderly woman sat in her rocker by a cheery fireplace. "I knew it was you by your step."

Karin was glad that Mrs. Larson was blind so she couldn't see her scowl. "Here's a fresh drink of water," she said, forcing a pleasant tone.

"Thank you, Karin. Oh me, oh my! My bones ache so when the weather is bad, I can hardly get around my own house. But the day has gone faster just knowing you'd be coming to read to me." Karin tucked the afghan around Mrs. Larson's stiff legs.

"Is that better?" she asked.

"Much—much better. You're a tonic for an old body like me." She clung to Karin's hand. "I know I'm a hard old woman, set in my ways and all. I've been thinking a lot today while I've been waiting for you. I've been hard on you, but you keep coming in spite of me. You're like the sun—" she cleared her throat. Karin was uncomfortable under this new Mrs. Larson, whose sharp tongue had often cut quite deeply. "I remember your beautiful gold curls before I went blind." She paused. "That book you were reading last time—go on with it."

Next morning Anna threw open Karin's bedroom door and snapped on the light. "Karin! Karin!" she exclaimed.

Karin hid her face in the pillow. "Go away and let me sleep," she mumbled.

Anna tugged at her shoulder. "Look at this paper." Karin raised up and opened one eye. Then the other eye popped open. Her own picture smiled back at her from the newspaper. "I don't believe it! I don't believe it! *Boden's Lucia is Karin Jacobson, nominated by Mrs. Eva Larson.*"

Roberta was kneeling on the bed beside Karin. "I could almost say, I told you so. Now I can be Lucia here at home with a clear conscience."

The morning of December 13th started very early. Karin helped Roberta dress for Lucia. How beautiful Roberta was in her white flowing dress with a red sash and her lingonberry wreath in which was set burning wax candles. The family sang: "Hail thee, Lucia, queen of light..."

Roberta laughed, "I never thought I'd hear Santa Lucia here in Sweden."

"Same tune but different words," Karin said. "Remember Lucia came from Sicily."

Roberta carried a silver tray of Lucia Cats and hot drinks to the family members. She and Karin had helped Mother to make the Lucia Cats which were buns shaped like cats' heads. Karin and her sisters, Anna and Margareta, were Roberta's attendants. They formed their own procession, carrying their goodies to neighbors and friends. Karin knew this was a day Roberta would remember forever.

Late that afternoon Karin found herself standing on the decorated truckbed waiting for the parade to start. The policemen, riding black horses, led the parade. Four runners followed the huge decorated truck which carried Lucia and her attendants as it rolled down the street. Karin wore a flowing white gown with a red sash. She felt elegant in a white fur coat and she held an armful of red poinsettias. The truck was also decked with the colorful flowers. Her attendants were dressed in white. On her head she wore the traditional crown of lingonberry leaves, but the candles were battery-powered to keep them burning. Next came the choirboys wearing white nightshirts over their street clothes and cone-shaped hats on their heads. The first boy carried the stars and the other choir members carried torches. They sang the melodious Lucia songs as they walked.

Santa Claus in his fur coat and red hat and belt was the last of the parade. His helpers were all dressed in gray suits with red belts and red hats.

The parade ended at the marketplace. Then Karin was taken to the assembly hall for the Lucia ball where the Mayor presented her with a beautiful silver necklace, which she could keep. The young men vied for the privilege of dancing with her. The evening was a whirl of unbelievable gaiety and popularity.

Late that night Karin and Roberta snuggled down under the covers. Karin pinched herself to make sure she hadn't been dreaming.

"Better get some shut-eye," Roberta said.

"Yes, it will be a busy time from now until Christmas, visiting hospitals, rest homes, and other public places and encouraging contributions for charity. And I'll have to work in reading time for Mrs. Larson. Who would have ever thought—" her voice trailed off.

Roberta mused, "Do you think there's ever been another home in all of Sweden where there's a Swedish and an American Lucia?"

What About Poinsettias?

In frigid Sweden, Lucia, the queen of the Festival of Lights, carries a bouquet of brilliant poinsettias, and poinsettias are used for her decorations. However, the poinsettia is really a tropical plant which grows abundantly in Central America and Mexico. It is also seen in parts of California.

Mexicans call it the **Holy Night Flower** *and* **Christmas Flower** *because it reaches its brightest red color only at Christmas. The plant grows wild, so even the poorest farmer can bring Christmas into his humble cottage. Every home and church is decorated with this Christmas Flower. Actually, the crimson petals are not a flower at all. Instead they are made of a cluster of colored leaves. The plant grows about ten feet high and has anywhere from twelve to thirty-six clusters of these burning leaves. Not until 1830 was this beautiful flower grown in North America.*

In 1810 a man by the name of Joel Roberts Poinsett was sent to South America by President James Madison. He was sent to Chile to watch the efforts of some rebels in that country who wished to break away from the Spanish rule. Mr. Poinsett loved freedom and thought people should not be ruled by kings. This made him unpopular with the governing royalty, and they called him "the scourge of the continent." Naturally he had to flee back to the United States.

Ten years later, President John Quincy Adams named him to be the first Minister to Mexico. Mexico was a country torn with rebellion and war. Mr. Poinsett sympathized with the rebels, so angry mobs stoned his home and shouted, "Out with Poinsett." In 1830 he returned to the United States, but this time he brought with him Mexico's native flower which he called "painted leaves."

Joel Poinsett was an amateur botanist with a very "green thumb." He hoped to develop a strong strain of this unusual plant so it could be enjoyed in the United States, where it was unknown. He lived in Charleston, South Carolina, and there, after much patient care, he developed a strong plant. He had many botanist friends. He sent these Christmas Flowers to many of them, much to their delight. Now the use of this spectacular plant has spread to Australia and South Africa, and even to Sweden, being cultivated in hothouses and nurseries.

The flower is very sensitive to light. Growers control the amount of light and darkness the plant gets. If it receives too much light, the blooming is delayed. Therefore, the plants are watched carefully so they will blossom at Christmas.

Mr. Poinsett died in 1851, feeling that his life as a diplomat was a failure. He had been named as a Secretary of War, but he was never remembered for his government service. However, one of his botanist friends, Robert Buist of Philadelphia, named the flaming flower for the man who brought it from Mexico in 1830. He called the plant the Poinsettia.

The Legend of the Flaming Flower

Long, long ago The Boy lived with his mother in Mexico in a small adobe hut. There were never enough pesos to buy food. Often The Boy went to bed hungry, and his mother was very sad. He wasn't big enough to hire out to men who needed help.

Christmas Eve was close at hand. He thought and thought of what he might take to the church to place before the statue of the Christ Child in memory of the night of his birth. With downcast eyes he watched for lost coins in the dust of the road, but no shiny object appeared. His friends talked of the gifts they would carry to the church, but he still could think of nothing.

"Mamacita[1], what can I take? The time is short and I must go with my friends to the church."

She shook her dark head sadly. "I have nothing. But you must go to worship on this important night. Perhaps no one will notice you do not carry a gift. There will be so many."

"But *I* will know and it hurts me deep inside."

"Go," the mother said.

Outside, his friends waited, carrying their tokens. "Where is yours?" one asked.

The Boy looked at the ground and kicked a rock with his toe. "My hands are empty." He shrugged his shoulders.

"Then you cannot go with us," the friends said. And off they trudged in the direction of the lighted church, leaving The Boy behind. The Boy dropped to a boulder by the road and wept bitterly. He buried his head in his hands. His tears soaked the ground. At last he wiped his eyes with the back of his hand, thinking he would go back home. What was Christmas Eve if he couldn't go to the big church? This was the greatest moment of the year, to put a gift at the feet of the Christ Child. Suddenly he blinked his eyes—again and again. He couldn't believe what he saw. At his feet, where his tears had dropped to the ground, a beautiful bright-red plant had suddenly grown.

"Here is my gift for the Christ Child. It is a miracle!" He stooped down and picked the flaming flowers and carried the plant to the church where he placed it among the gifts. It was so brilliant that all the people gasped at its beauty.

That Christmas Eve The Boy went home with a singing, happy heart. He had no way of knowing that he had presented a gift that would live on and on in his beloved land. The flaming Christmas flower would thrill the hearts of his countrymen and they, too, would carry his flowers as gifts to the Christ Child.

---

[1]Pronounced Mah-mah-SEE-tah, meaning mother

What About
Santa Claus?
R. Palmer

In Holland, December 5th is St. Nicholas Eve and December 6th is St. Nicholas Day. This is gift-giving day and a day for parties and celebrations. The religious side of the Christmas season is saved for December 25th. Christmas Eve and Day are spent in going to church services and for family gatherings around the fireside.

But where did Santa Claus come from?

Nicholas of Myra lived in the fourth century and Nicholas of Pinora died in 564. Both of these men were important in history and were known for their good deeds. They have been combined through the years into one symbol, **St. Nicholas** *or* **Sinterklaas.** *Legends state that St. Nicholas dropped gifts down the chimney into wooden shoes set by the fireplace for deserving poor people and for children. Legends also say that he chained the devil and took him along on his leaps from roof to roof. The devil became known as Black Peter. Black Peter punishes the bad children and* **Sinterklaas** *rewards the good.*

When the Dutch people came to America, of course they brought **Sinterklaas** *as a part of their Christmas tradition. The English brought with them* **Father Christmas,** *who was a roly-poly, jolly fellow in high boots. In the course of time these two came together in one symbol—Santa Claus—in a red suit and pointed cap and white beard. Americans changed Santa Claus so that he came on Christmas Eve, bringing his gifts for Christmas socks.*

In Germany long ago the Christ Child brought the gifts. He was known as **Christkindel.** *From that name,* **Kriss Kringle** *was attached to a jolly figure who has brought the gifts for German children.*

In France, **Père Noël** *deposited gifts in the wooden shoes of peasants.*

In 1809 Washington Irving's story of St. Nicholas was published in his **Knickerbocker History** *which was circulated in England and America. Then in 1821* **The Children's Friend,** *a small children's book, was published. It had eight sparkling colored pictures and eight verses about* **Santeclaus.** *He was shown riding in a sleigh drawn by a single reindeer. This is probably the first time Santa Claus appeared with a reindeer.*

A few years later, Dr. Clement Moore, an Episcopal preacher in New York, wrote **A Visit from St. Nicholas** *for his own children. The story was based on his own family and their surroundings. This poem is familiar to young and old and has shaped one picture of Santa Claus and his eight reindeer. This poem probably would never have gone beyond the Moore fireside. However, a friend, Miss Harriet Butler, was visiting the Moores that Christmas. She received permission to copy it in her album, and the following year it was published anonymously in* **The Troy Sentinel.** *Strangely, that same year, 1837, Robert W. Weir, professor of art at West Point, painted a portrait of Santa Claus, fat and jolly, ready to go up the chimney after filling the stockings. The picture, being published at the same time, served to make the Santa Claus of the new poem very real.*

But whether it be **Santa Claus** *in America,* **Sinterklaas** *in Holland,* **Joulupukki** *in Finland,* **JulTomten** *in Sweden,* **Kriss Kringle** *in Germany,* **Père Noël** *in France, or* **Father Christmas** *in England, one word symbolizes them all—GENEROSITY. And that, after all, is the spirit which makes Christmas. Yes, there* **is** *a Santa Claus!*

How Christmas Came To Be

(Written by Vonna Noyes at age 9)

In the magic land of the North Pole dwelt some very, very special people. They were special because they had the gift to perform magic. This was because they were good and lived the Savior's golden rule. Even though the men were tiny, with misshapen bodies and homely faces, they were a pleasure to look upon, because of the goodness that glowed from within, (Others called them elves or brownies.) Their womenfolk also were tiny, but truly beautiful to see. (All the girls wished they could look and be like the fairies.)

They loved their neighbors as they loved themselves, and were always so busy doing thoughtful acts that there was no time or place for unhappiness, greed, or discontent in their country.

Jolly Elf and Holly Fairy were happily planning their honeymoon, for they were to be married soon. They thought it would be exciting to find out what lay in the world beyond them.

As the day arrived, excitement was in the air. Their friends and neighbors filled the sleigh with food, clothing, and other necessities. Prancer, Dasher, Donner, Blitzen and Comet were anxious to be under way.

Up, up, into the clear blue sky, out over the housetops they flew. How big the houses were; the people were giants.

"Is it safe to land down there? Everything is so big," said Holly.

"We've got to take that chance to find out how those creatures live down there," said Jolly. They saw a small clearing in a schoolyard and landed. Things had looked big from the sky, but now they were huge.

They heard:

"Billy Moore, give me my jumping rope this very minute!"

"Ah, try and get it," yelled Billy, taking off on the run. "You're just a stupid ole girl and you can't catch me." He almost stepped on poor Jolly, who suddenly jumped aside.

"Boy! We had better get away from here," Jolly said to Holly.

Hurrying from the schoolyard, they reached the street just in time to see two men with stockings over their faces and holding banging things in their hands, running from a building with the word *Bank* written over the door. Giant people were scattering in every direction. Three of them fell on the ground. Giants

---

This story won honorable mention in the Junior Writers' Contest sponsored by the League of Utah Writers in 1970.

dressed in white drove up in a big, white, wailing thing with a flashing red light on top. The men in white picked up the fallen giants and put them in the big, white object, then drove away.

Walking down the street, they overheard people talking about their troubles, others quarreling. "This is terrible," said Holly. "These giants need to learn love, one for another. Let's get out of here and go home. Perhaps our friends can help us think of something to make these poor creatures happy." So back to the schoolyard they went, into their sleigh, then up and away.

Oh, it was wonderful to get back to the sweet, quiet, wonderful land of love. They rang the churchbell. Everyone came running, for naturally they wanted to know about the world outside. Jolly and Holly told them of their adventure and asked for suggestions to help these giants to have love and consideration for each other.

Grandpa Santa Claus said, "Let's make toys and candy and take them to the home of each child while he is sleeping."

Happy Elf said, "That's a good idea, but it isn't teaching them the joy of giving, only the joy of receiving."

Grandma Claus said, "Our Savior taught us to love one another. Let's make it a day to honor him—his birthday."

Jolly said, "Good. We could leave a storybook about our Savior's birth for everyone to read about his teachings. Then they would learn to be kind and do good things for each other."

Holly said, "We're forgetting something. No one knows the true date of our Savior's birth. The good book doesn't tell us."

"Well," said Grandpa Claus, "we can choose a day and make it in memory of his birth anyway."

"Sure we can," Holly said. "Let's put all the days of the year in a hat, then draw one. It should be a winter day so we can use our sleigh and our flying reindeer."

"Okay," said Jolly, "we will use only the winter months. Tinker Bell, draw the date from the hat."

"The 25th of December. That's a real good date," said Tinker Bell. "Our deer won't have any trouble getting around then."

Vixen said, "We reindeer have an idea, too. Let's cut and decorate pine trees and put presents under them."

"Oh, that's a wonderful idea!" said the fairies. "Yes, and we'll need a leader to take the gifts around each year. The rest of us will build and sew things. It will keep us busy the whole year through."

Jolly said, "Grandpa Claus is so fat and jolly; he can organize and deliver our gifts. With our magic flying deer, it shouldn't take more than one night's work. We can all help to load the sleigh and make sure no one is missed."

No one has as much fun or enjoys life as much as Grandpa and Grandma Santa Claus and the wee people, for they give joy and love to millions of earth people.

The giant people call it CHRISTMAS.

Scout Sub

Since I was Senior Patrol Leader, I stood at the door of the old log Scout house. "Wipe your feet on that rug!" I warned, as each boy entered. I looked down at my uniform. My trouser legs were almost mid-calf. My scout shirt sleeves hadn't met my wrists for ages and the shirt was faded with age. I felt self-conscious in it, but I couldn't bug my parents for a new uniform now that I was almost ready for Exploring. If only I could finish those Eagle requirements.

I surveyed the big log room with pride. It was really great that our troop[1] could hold meetings in a log cabin over seventy-five years old. Believe me, we took pride in keeping it up, too. Outside, the wind and snow were blowing hard, but the cabin was snug. A crackling fire burned in the rock fireplace at one end of the big room.

At eight sharp I called the boys to attention for posting of the colors. Inspection and other preliminaries followed. We were lucky to have Joe and Meredith Palmer for our scoutmasters. Joe was tall—I guess you could call him down-right handsome. He was graying at the temples. His big voice boomed out occasionally over our hub-bub. You can't very well have a Scout meeting without noise. The Scout quiet sign was raised several times and picked up by the boys so that troop business could be transacted.

After a fast game of *Around the Chair*, to get rid of the wiggles, we plopped on the floor in front of the blackboard. The Green Bar announced the next matter of business, which included instructions and necessary preparations for an overnight winter camp. This was Meredith Palmer's department. After showing us actual examples of different kinds of packs, he told us a lot about the art of packing. He said, "Of course, you little guys can't pack much in your extra pair of pants. But *mine*—" We all roared. Meredith was several handspans across. "Why, I could pack *everything* in mine."

The lights were turned off and we made the rafters ring with song. You'd never believe how much real music Meredith could get out of us around a roaring fire when the wind howls outside.

After the other guys had gone, I stayed behind. I was almost afraid to bring up my idea for a service project, which was the only thing keeping me from my Eagle. I sort of hung around, cleaning up, not knowing how to jump into the subject. Joe was gathering up papers at the table. He looked up and said, "Mark Severin, when are you ever going to move on your service project?" I was glad he broke the ice.

---

[1] Troop 108, Lakeshore District, Bountiful, Utah

"That's exactly what I want to talk to you about," I said. Meredith sat down with Joe and I sat on the floor, hugging my knees. "During the Thanksgiving weekend, I talked it over with my family. I want to sub for Santa."

They glanced at each other. Meredith shook his head and waggled his finger at me. "You're too skinny, boy. I know—you really want *me* to stand in for you. Right?" He patted his ample middle.

"Hadn't thought of that," I laughed.

"Too bad I don't have a Santa suit." Meredith slapped his knee.

"You'd make a neat Santa Claus at that—no padding necessary." I ducked my head because it was the truth, but I wasn't sure how he'd take it.

Their laughter almost shook the antlers of the deerhead mounted on the crossbeams above. Then they were sober. "How do you propose to earn money for a thing like this? You're not loaded—we know that. Are you sure you haven't got a tiger by the tail?" Joe asked.

I gulped. "How did you know what I'd planned to do?" I asked.

"What do you mean?"

"Well—that 'tiger by the tail' bit—I had planned to rent the Disney film *The Tiger Walks.* Thought I could get permission to use the cultural hall in the church building. I figure this is a community project. You know, the townspeople would be helping by coming to the movie. Here's a sample of a ticket I've typed." It read:

The Tiger Walks
December 15th
Suggested Contributions:
Adults 75¢ Children 35¢

I went on, "I'd sell popcorn and candy to make extra money. The proceeds would provide Christmas for a family. I figure I'd learn a lot in a service project of this kind."

"A whole lot!" Joe nodded. "What happens if you don't have a good turnout for the movie and don't make much money?"

"Don't say that. It has to succeed. The troop could sell tickets and put up chairs and help sell popcorn and candy that night and it would make them a part of the project. In a way they'd be giving of themselves this Christmas."

"What about a prospective family?" Meredith asked.

"Mom called the South Davis Community Council for a family."

"You know this will take your own Christmas?" Joe warned.

"Sure. But it'll be Christmas enough, if I can do a good job of this. I never realized that there are people who wouldn't have any Christmas if someone didn't sub. Sounds fun to me."

Joe nodded, "We're behind you all the way, Mark. I think you've got a great idea."

The next two weeks were busy ones. Even in school I found myself worrying over all the details. What if people wouldn't come to the movie? It cost $27.50 to rent the movie, and that would have to come out of the profit. I swallowed hard every time I thought of that little detail. Selling tickets was a pretty discouraging business. Everyone was too busy to listen. One Saturday I tramped from door to door for four long hours without selling a ticket. I learned one thing—I'm no salesman. But it was hard to smile and be enthusiastic without any encouragement. I felt like the smile was frozen on my face.

Grandma and Grandpa ran a small neighborhood bakery, so they kept a jar on the counter by the cash register and explained my project to their customers. When the coins stacked up in the jar, Grandma exchanged them for green money and it looked like the jar needed some help again. With that and advance ticket sales, I had enough to pay for movie rental.

A local newspaper did an article on my project and took some pictures. It made me feel important. At school, I almost enjoyed the razzing of the kids: "Hi, Santa Claus!" "Good ole Sub!" It was great to be "neat."

The night of the movie was crisp and cold—a perfect night for everyone to be enjoying a fireplace at home. Mom and my sisters Brenda, Karen, and Jeanette had popped and sacked corn to be sold. I was sick inside when I saw that mostly kids sauntered into the recreation hall. Tonight I had to earn enough for my family. But kids don't have much money, especially before Christmas, I thought. I'd probably carry home the popcorn and candy I intended to sell. Not many of my school friends showed up. That really shafted me. I felt like hiding behind the velvet curtains on the stage. I'd go broke for sure and what would happen to my Christmas family? But by the time the movie started, there was a fair-sized audience—and they all bought.

That night when I counted my haul, I had over $70 profit. What really surprised me was that later, at church, people occasionally shook my hand and left money in it—for my project, they said.

The agency assigned me a family consisting of a mother and her two children—a boy four and a girl six. Mom went with me to get acquainted and to see what they needed. When Mrs. Smith answered the door, I knew something was wrong. She had such a puzzled look. She brushed her hand across her forehead and said, "But I thought only rich people did this. And they've sent a boy!" Jiminy Christmas! I was afraid she was going to cry.

Mom took over and said, "I'm sure we can provide a good Christmas for your children. What do they need?"

"Oh dear! Oh, we'll get along. We really don't need a thing."

Who did she think she was kidding? "Do you have Christmas tree ornaments," I ventured. What a lame question!

"Oh, we don't need a thing," she insisted. Now how did she think we could do anything if we didn't know what to do?

Mom talked to her on the phone a few times, trying to wheedle some information out of her, and learned that she was a very independent little woman. She'd recently been divorced; she'd had a heart attack and a stack of other troubles. She really needed a lift with Christmas, but she wouldn't say how. It was a good thing Mom was such a good shopper and knew what they might need—I think they call it woman's intuition, or something like that. And could she ever stretch my dollars when we went shopping.

At school, I was given a tree for my family, but trimmings were expensive. A friend donated ornaments and icicles and I bought the lights. Christmas was a hair away and Mom asked, "Mark, what do you want for Christmas?"

"Nothing at all," I said, and I meant it. "You've helped me so much. I never realized before how much time and money it takes to have things under a Christmas tree."

The day before Christmas I bought the turkey and all the trimmings for Christmas dinner. Mrs. Smith still wouldn't tell me what she needed. I had $5 left, and I decided to give her the money, along with a box of chocolates which I bought out of my own money. I delivered everything to the Smiths and dragged myself home. Christmas Eve I went to bed with such a gnawing feeling in my stomach, I was sure it was an ulcer. I hadn't done enough for them. I'd really goofed. Whatever made me think I could tackle a project like this in the first place? Would the little kids be happy?

Christmas morning I was awake before anyone else, but not because I expected to find anything for myself. I just plain hadn't slept. But I knew I had to make the best of things. "Merry Christmas!" I shouted. My "ulcer" was gone and I did feel better. Under our own tree I found a *Swinger* camera with my name on it. Just what I wanted! Excitement ran high at our house, but my thoughts were with the Smiths.

Suddenly the telephone rang. I picked up the receiver and shouted, "Merry Christmas!"

"Santa?" Mrs. Smith asked, a catch in her voice. Jiminy Christmas! She sounded like she was going to cry again.

"Yes?" I was so anxious I almost climbed through the phone. All I heard was silence! Now I knew I'd failed.

"I—" More silence. "I just want you to know that a boy has given us the most wonderful Christmas we've ever had."

"Whoopee!" I couldn't help it. But I could hear the kids clamoring to talk to Santa Claus. Hey, that was me! I couldn't believe how excited and happy they were. Jiminy Christmas! I caught myself wiping my eyes with the back of my hand. Why, this was the most fun of my whole life. I decided this was what Christmas was all about.

I'd finished earning my Eagle in the process. I had learned something else, too. I knew why they always give a guy's mother an Eagle pin along with the Scout.

What About Gift-giving?

As related in the Gospel according to St. Matthew, the wisemen followed the star to Bethlehem where they found the Christ Child living in a house with Mary and Joseph. This event is supposed to have taken place twelve days after the birth of the Savior, and is called Epiphany.[1]

A legend in Italy states that Befana[2] *sat inside her little cottage toasting her shins before her cozy fire. Outside the wind howled, and a storm was blowing up. How happy she was that she didn't have to go out on such a night. Suddenly she was surprised by a knock at her door. As she opened her door a crack and peeped out, she saw three men in fine robes and turbans.*

"Can you tell us the way to Bethlehem? We are trying to find the Christ Child. Will you go with us and help us find the way?"

Befana refused to go with them. After all, what could an old woman do in the storm? So the Wisemen continued on their way.

Befana returned to her cozy flame, but at last her conscience got the best of her and she set out to find the Wisemen. And, in turn, the Christ Child. However, she never caught up with them. At Ephiphany she flies from house to house on a broomstick. Legend says that she goes into the houses dressed in shabby clothes and looks at the faces of the children, trying to find the right one. As she goes, she rewards good children by leaving gifts in their stockings. She is the gift-giver in Italy. But for the bad children, she leaves a switch and a piece of coal.

The Russians have an old Grandmother very much like **Befana,** *whom they call* **Baboushka.**[3] *The same legend is told to Russian children about her.*

In Holland wooden shoes are placed by the fireside to receive the gifts from **Sinterklaas** *on December 6th.*

In France, before going to bed on Christmas Eve, the children set their shoes by the fireside, hoping for a gift from **Père Noël**. *Many years ago peasants wore wooden shoes, called* **sabots**. *So they put out wooden shoes as the Dutch did. Today ordinary shoes are used. But the pastry shops make chocolate wooden shoes and fill them with candies, which recalls the old wooden-shoe custom.*

Christmas stockings became a part of the English tradition, because one Christmas Eve **Father Christmas** *dropped some gold coins down a chimney. Ordinarily the coin would have dropped into the grate. But this time it dropped into a stocking which had been left by the fireside to dry. Ever since then,* **Father Christmas** *is expected to fill the stockings which have been hung up for him.*

This custom of hanging stockings, was carried to America by the English immigrants.

---

[1]Pronounced E-PIF-fuh-nee
[2]Pronounced Buh-FAH-nuh
[3]Pronounced Buh-BOOSH-ka

Amy's Awakening

Ugh! I hate practicing!" Amy groaned, as she slammed shut the lid of the violin case.

Uncle Sam was maneuvering his wheelchair into the living room. He asked, "What's that all about?"

"Oh, why do I have to practice, practice, practice!" she stormed.

"Aren't you going to play for the family Christmas program tonight?"

"Of course." Amy popped into the armchair.

"I remember an old proverb, 'There is no excellence without labor,'" he said slowly. "Nothing sounds worse than a squeaky violin, and it takes practice to play without squeaks."

"Do you know how hard it is?" Amy asked.

"Yes, I used to play the violin. Oh, how I wanted one of my own."

"Well, why didn't you get one?"

"We didn't even have enough money for what we needed, so I never got one. I played my father's. But it wasn't *mine*! I remember a Christmas—long ago—" Uncle Sam's good eye became misty.

Amy pulled the footstool over to the wheelchair and looked into the kindly, wrinkled face. He's so old; he has only one eye and only one leg, but it's like sitting in the sunshine to be around him, she thought. "Tell me about it," she urged.

"Well, it happened eighty-eight years ago when I was ten. Father and I went to the canyon to find our own Christmas tree—a beautiful cedar. We brought it home and put it in the corner of the kitchen which was our living room, too. Then we popped popcorn which we strung on thread."

"You mean, the fluffy popcorn we *eat*?"

"Yes—it looked so pretty against the green. We made molasses syrup for the leftover corn and had popcorn balls. Mama snapped candles onto the ends of the branches. Why, it was as pretty as your tree in the corner—no, even prettier," he teased. "A few days before Christmas I rummaged through my socks and discovered they all had holes in the toes. I complained to Mama. She promised that if I would help with all the Christmas preparations, she would knit me a new sock to hang up. I did everything she asked and everything she didn't ask, but still she didn't have time to knit that sock. We didn't have fancy felt socks like all of yours hanging from the mantel.

This story is based on a true incident in the life of Samuel C. Dutson who, at ninety-eight, is still playing his harmonica.

"So I hung up my worn sock and went to bed with a heavy heart because I knew if I got any hard tack, it would slip right through that holey toe. Christmas morning we all rushed to see what our socks held. Would you believe it! There was a brand new sock with my name on it. Mama was a fast knitter and she had stayed up all night knitting so I wouldn't be disappointed. In my sock was an apple, an orange, five pieces of hardtack and right in the toe was a mouth organ. I put it to my mouth and ran it between my lips. What a thrill! Mama said, 'Now, Sam, I hope you'll play that mouth organ every single day.' My, it was a privilege to *own* an instrument—even a mouth organ. And I'm still practicing—at ninety-eight! I'd better get busy now if I'm going to play for the family program tonight," he winked.

Uncle Sam reached into his shirt pocket and drew out a small case from which he haltingly lifted a harmonica. "My breath is kinda short now and my hands shake, but I still can bring happiness to people with my music."

"Is that the same harmonica?" Amy asked.

"Oh my, no! I've worn out several in eighty-eight years. I couldn't count the programs I've played for in that time. People used to say I could make them think they were listening to a whole orchestra. There's a thrill that comes from uplifting others with your gift that nothing else brings."

"Uncle Sam, will you play with me?" Amy hesitated.

"Of course. Let's do *Silent Night* to warm up."

Amy tuned her violin and they played it through once. Then she slipped the mute over the strings for the second verse. As the soft tones came from her violin harmonizing with the harmonica, Amy experienced a new thrill. She was part of an orchestra and together they were telling the Christmas story. "Will you play with me often, Uncle Sam? For the first time I feel the music—you've given me a real Christmas gift. I'll try harder now."

"I've only awakened the gift that was already in you—asleep. You have it, Amy girl, and now *you* can give it away all *your* life. Practice will perfect the gift." A tear of happiness rolled down the wrinkled old cheek.

"And *you* are still giving it away at ninety-eight!" Amy planted a kiss on his cheek.

What About
Shepherds?

The shepherds of Palestine have changed very little down through the centuries. Even today the shepherd can be seen on the hills or on the road at the head of his flock. Often he carries a tired lamb or a hurt sheep over his shoulder. His face is usually burned almost black from the hot sun. He wears a flowing head-veil which is held on with two black, twisted cords. Beneath his robes he often wears a sheepskin coat with the fleece turned next to his body.

The shepherd loves and understands his flock. He never drives the sheep, but always leads them to new pasture. He often talks to them in a loud sing-song voice, which sounds more animal than human, in a strange succession of sounds. But his sheep understand and they know his voice. The sheep dog is there, not to drive the flock, but to help protect the sheep from wolves and other wild animals. When two flocks spend the night together on the hills, the shepherds separate in the morning and call their own sheep to them, and the flock follows the right shepherd. To watch this is to understand what the Savior meant when he said: "My sheep shall know my voice. I am the good shepherd, and know my sheep and am known of mine."

Candy canes are a part of our modern Christmas. They should remind us of the staff of the faithful shepherd who visited the Savior on the night of his birth.

Joel, the Shepherd Boy

Joel gazed into the night sky with wonder. A strange glow dimmed the brightness of the stars. An uneasy feeling held him and he shuddered. In the distance he heard a faint howl. That was no dog! He looked back. Why had Abner sent him alone, without a dog, to search for his lost lamb, Tiny? The glow in the sky told him this was no ordinary night. Yes, he was afraid. He admitted it.

He stood still, leaning on his shepherd's staff, and listened intently. No sound. He couldn't even hear the sheep over the hill—or was it two hills away? He couldn't remember, but his legs were so weary. He lifted his goatskin waterbag to his lips and took a sip. How could the little animal have wandered this far? He cupped his hand to his mouth so that his strange, animal-like call would travel farther. Again he listened. He was glad he had hung the bell around Tiny's neck just that morning. But no tinkle broke the stillness. Again the howl came, closer this time. He hurried on, grateful that the sky's glow also lighted the ground somewhat. At least he wasn't so apt to stumble and fall over unseen rocks and boulders. Again he heard the howl pierce the air, this time much closer. What was that other sound? Was it? Yes, it was the faintest tinkling of a bell. His heart skipped a beat, and he ran in the direction of the soft sound. Suddenly he was at the edge of a stone ledge. He peered anxiously into the darkness.

"Maa-aa!" and the tinkle of the moving bell sounded close by. Joel almost laughed at that unusual, high-pitched "Maa-aa!". None but Tiny bleated like that. But now the howl of the wolf seemed dangerously close. Again he strained his eyes, searching, searching. "Maa-aa," Joel bleated, hoping to get a response from the lamb. "Maa-aa!" rose from below and to his right. "There you are, little one," Joel said. "I found you at last. Now how will I get you up off that ledge? You've been gone a long time. You must be hungry."

Joel looked at his staff. "You're too far down to reach you with the crook of my staff. If I could get you to hang onto something. I know! My sash!" Quickly Joel unwound his long sash from his waist. "That wolf must smell you miles off. He's coming in our direction sure, Tiny. He's had too many of our sheep lately. But he's not going to get you, if I can help it. If you could catch the end of the sash in your mouth, I could pull you up." Joel dropped the fabric down the ledge, but the slight breeze carried it away from the lamb. He drew it back up. "Now what shall I do? There's no time to spare."

He picked up a small stone, not too big for the lamb's tiny mouth, and slipped it into a worn spot of the double thickness of cloth. It slid to the very tip of the sewed sash. Good! Then he soaked the end in water from the goatskin. Tiny would be thirsty—he might hang onto that wet sash to get some water. It was his only hope. Now maybe it will reach him, Joel thought. He slid the sash over the edge of the ledge right above the lamb, and dangled it. "Maa-aa!" the lamb bleated. But the sound was cut off by the howl, closer, closer. The hair stood up on Joel's neck. He was terrified.

"Hurry! Grab it!" Joel pleaded, dangling it just above the lamb's mouth. As if understanding the urgency, the lamb opened his mouth and closed it around the heavy, wet end. As Joel hoped, the lamb began sucking the wet sash and rock. Joel tugged slowly and gently, but his arms were taut and he held his breath lest he should be too slow to pull Tiny to safety. He knew too well that if Tiny opened his mouth, he would plunge down, down into the black ravine. That would be the end of Tiny, because the sides were so steep and sharp he'd never be able to climb down the ravine. He imagined he could hear the heavy panting of the wolf. Joel pulled the lamb-attached sash almost to the top. Now he grabbed his staff with one hand and scooped the lamb into the crook. With one quick jerk, he had Tiny in his arms. The panting sound stopped and Joel could see the gleaming eyes of the wolf and his outline poised to leap. With a sharp crack, Joel caught the wolf in mid-air with his staff, throwing the animal off balance. Straight down the ravine, that wolf sailed with an eerie howl that echoed from its yawning depths.

Joel picked up his bent, cracked staff. "You did your job well that time, old staff." He shook his head sadly. "I don't know where I'll get another one as good as you've been." Still cradling the lamb in his arms, he reached down to pick up his sash.

What was that sound? That was no wolf—it was music—singing! He straightened and turned in the direction of the chanting voices. He'd been so intent on saving Tiny, he hadn't realized that the sky's glow had brightened. He blinked his eyes, thinking he must be dreaming. Inside the bright glow he could make out figures. Were these angels? They had to be. Nothing else could be in the sky. He'd never heard such heavenly music. It touched him deeply and he was suddenly aware of tears streaming down his face. The words! What were they singing?

"Glory to God in the Highest;
And on earth peace, good will toward men."

He watched as the heavenly choir rose upward and finally disappeared. And when they were gone away Joel could see a brilliant star in the east, in the direction of Bethlehem.

"Tiny, we must find Abner and see what is the meaning of all this!" He put his lamb between his legs to hold it and wrapped his sash around and around his waist. Then he picked up the lamb and his broken staff and began to run in the direction from whence he had come. Over the hill, and the next hill, and he could see the flock sleeping on the ground with Abner sitting on a boulder, his face turned to the sky.

"Abner! Abner!" Joel fell to his knees exhausted. "What does it mean?"

"You saw?" Abner's browned, wrinkled face glowed.

"I saw many angels and I heard them singing 'Peace on earth, good will to men.'" Joel's words tumbled over each other.

"It is prophecy fulfilled, Joel. The promised Messiah has come. We were watching the flocks and lo, the angel of the Lord came upon us and the glory of the Lord shone round about us and we were sore afraid. But the angel said unto us, Fear not, for behold I bring you good tidings of great joy. For unto you is born this day, in the city of David, a Savior which is Christ, the Lord. And this shall be a sign unto you. Ye shall find the babe wrapped in swaddling clothes and lying in a manger. And suddenly there was with the angel, a multitude of the heavenly hosts, praising God and saying, Glory to God in the Highest and on earth peace, good will toward men. You heard them, Joel. You know I speak the truth, do you not?" Abner's shining eyes searched Joel's upturned face. Joel nodded. "The others went to find him. I stayed behind," Abner continued, "to watch the flock and to wait for you. You found your lamb, I see."

Joel hugged Tiny to him tightly. "I'll never let him go."

"Maa-aa," the lamb bleated his treble tones, and the bell tinkled. Joel laughed and squeezed him. "He'd fallen onto a ledge. The wolf almost got him, Abner. That wolf will never bother us again. He's in the bottom of the ravine." Joel showed Abner his broken staff. "It saved my lamb and me."

"If you follow the star, Joel, it will guide you to the stable where the babe lies in swaddling clothes in a manger. I know it will be a great sacrifice, but should you not take your lamb as a gift for the Child?"

"No. Tiny is mine. How can I part with him, after I've saved his life?"

"Go, my boy, and see the Savior. It is a privilege for only a few. You have heard the angels. I am old. But you are young and you shall tell many of this night. Our people have waited long for a king to deliver us from bondage. But the prophet Isaiah has said, 'He shall feed his flocks, like a shepherd, and he shall gather the lambs to his fold.' Bring me word. I must stay with the sheep."

It was almost morning when Joel stood at the entrance of the cave. The brilliant light of the star had faded almost into day. A bearded man with a kind face beckoned Joel inside. "Come, you may see the child."

The woman raised herself from the pile of straw where she lay beside the manger. "Another shepherd?" she smiled. "Come."

Joel moved slowly toward her. She was holding the baby in her arms. He gazed in awe at the beautiful child. I would do anything for this Child, Joel thought. He looked lovingly at Tiny. "Here, here is my lamb. A gift for the baby," Joel said, and his heart was light. As he knelt beside the manger, he laid down his staff and was suddenly embarrassed that it was broken. "I know not why I brought a broken staff, except that it has saved my life and my lamb's," Joel fumbled.

"Take your lamb with you," the woman smiled. "The giving is important and you have willingly offered what was dearest to you. As for your broken staff, leave it; for my son will have the power to mend a broken staff. His staff will reach out to save not only sheep, but all mankind."

What About
Carols?
A. Palmer

From the Christmas story in the Gospel according to St. Luke, we read that "suddenly there was with the angel a multitude of the heavenly hosts, praising God and saying: Glory to God in the Highest and on earth peace, Good Will toward men." The first Christmas carols were sung by angels.

The spontaneous efforts of human beings fall far short of that first group of singers, but the spirit of good will toward men can compensate for the lack.

The custom of caroling is growing in America. In some cities formal groups of singers walk through the streets singing the old carols. In Santa Barbara, California, for instance, bands of singers dress in flowing red capes and peaked hoods, bringing cheer to the lonely and homebound as well as friends and neighbors. More and more young people are learning the thrill of dropping in on shut-ins to leave their happiness in song.

Perhaps **Silent Night** *is the most popular of all Christmas carols. How did it come to be written?*

High in a valley of the Austrian Alps, it was Christmas Eve, 1818, in the little village of Oberndorf. Father Joseph Mohr, the twenty-six-year-old village priest, sat alone in his study preparing his sermon for Christmas Day. He was interrupted by a knock at the door. A peasant woman pleaded with him to come to the house of a poor charcoal-maker where a newborn baby needed a blessing from the priest. After a long, hard climb up the mountain in the bitter cold, the big awkward father ushered Father Mohr into the crude, poorly-lighted hut. There the mother lay on a hard bed with the baby in her arms. After performing the rite, Father Mohr started back down the mountain. Below him lay the valley, dotted by the lights of many rush lamps carried by the mountaineers on their way to church. He completed Midnight Mass, then went to his study where he tried to put down on paper what had happened to him. He hoped this might be his Christmas sermon for it reminded him of that memorable night almost two thousand years ago. But the words kept turning into verse.

As a young orphan, studying at St. Peter's, he had dreamed of becoming a poet and musician. He had a beautiful tenor voice and he had loved music more than anything else. But his foster father, the Very Reverend Father Hiernle, insisted that he be a priest, and he shortly found himself as the vicar of a tumble-down church in Oberndorf.

Franz Xaver Gruber was the new teacher in the village. He was five years older than Father Mohr and had an impressive bass voice. He played the guitar and was also organist for the church. The two enjoyed making music together. The village children often stood before the manse and nudged one another, saying, "Listen, the priest and the teacher are singing again."

These two men had been friends for two years before this particular Christmas, when Father Mohr wrote his poem. Christmas morning he took his poem to Gruber who was so pleased with it that he immediately wrote a tune to fit the words. Mice had eaten a hole in the bellows of the church organ, so it could not be used. But Father Mohr and Franz Gruber delighted the congregation that Christmas Day by singing the new song they had written with guitar accompaniment.

From the Zillertal, a valley in a neighboring Austrian province, came Karl

Mauracher, the organ builder. After repairing the church organ, he turned to Franz Gruber and asked, "Want to try it, Mr. Gruber?" Without even realizing it, Franz Gruber began to play **Silent Night**, *and he and Father Mohr were singing it for the organ builder.*

Karl Mauracher was delighted with the new song and asked for it. "I will gladly give it to you," Father Mohr said. The organ builder said it would be unnecessary to write it down—he would carry it in his head with a hundred other songs that were already there. Over the mountains to the Zillertal, he sang it, pleasing the people along the way with the new song. Somewhere along the way he forgot the last two verses. At home in the Zillertal, the four Strasser children, Caroline, Sepp, Andearl, and Maly, loved to sing and they picked up the song from the organ builder. Of course, they had no idea where the song came from, and they called it a **Song from Heaven**. *This song brought fame to the Strasser children, and finally they sang many concerts throughout the land. Always they sang the* **Song from Heaven** *to begin every concert. It seems to possess strange, almost-magical qualities. Fourteen years from the date it was written, they sang it for the King and Queen. When the King asked where the* **Song from Heaven** *came from, they told him it was a folk song. After all, they had no idea of its origin.*

The King had his Berlin cathedral choir sing the song often. However, the choir was made up chiefly of Army recruits, detailed to singing duty. And they put a distinctly military flavor to it. It found its way into the Prussian hymn book as **Silent Night**. *Below the caption was: "Author and Composer unknown." This disturbed the King. He ordered his Royal Concertmaster, Ludwig Erk, to find out who had written it. Master Erk travelled and searched without success, and finally decided that Michael Haydn, a brother of Joseph Haydn of Vienna, must have written it, although there was no proof. He started home, afraid to admit his failure to the King. On the way he stopped at an inn. In the corner a bullfinch warbled a sweet tune. Suddenly he sat up. "The bird! He is singing my song! Where did you get him?" he demanded.*

"A traveler left him," the innkeeper said. "The man said he had bought the bird in Salzburg in St. Peter's Abbey."

Master Erk immediately went to St. Peter's Abbey. But there he was informed that the bullfinch couldn't have come from their Abbey, since they felt it was sinful to train birds to sing songs other than that which the Almighty had given them to sing. However, the choir inspector, Ambrosius Prennsteiner, knew his choir boys well. People paid good money for trained birds, and it was entirely possible that a choir boy was making a little money on the side by training bullfinches to sing. So he secretly posted himself outside the window and with a leaf before his lips, he whistled **Silent Night**. *He was justly proud of his imitation of a bullfinch. Then he heard a boy inside yell, "Hey, you—your bird has come back!" A moment later, he spied one of his nine-year-old choir boys creeping around the corner on tiptoe, ready to catch his singing bird. It was Felix Gruber. Seeing the choirmaster, Felix bent over to receive his punishment from the baton Mr. Prennsteiner held.*

"Where did you get that song?" Mr. Prennsteiner inquired, without giving the customary discipline.

"From my father, of course. He made it up. He is the choirmaster and organist in Hallein."

Within a matter of hours, Felix Gruber found himself presenting Mr. Prennsteiner to his parents at home. Mr. Prennsteiner said to the father, Franz Gruber, "I hear you have not only produced this promising scion, you have also written a very famous song. It's that beautiful Christmas song of yours, you know **Silent Night.***"*

"Why, I wrote that when I was just a village teacher in Oberndorf, thirty-five years ago," Mr. Gruber said.

His wife Marie added, "We always sing it on Christmas Eve and Franz has taught it to all our children."

"You may be interested to know it's in the Prussian hymn book—author and composer unknown," Mr. Prennsteiner explained.

"Does the Prussian know the right words?" Gruber asked. "The words aren't mine. They were written by the late Father Mohr. There are six beautiful stanzas. By the way, he went to school at your St. Peter's too."

"Well," said Mr. Prennsteiner, "our Prussian knew only four stanzas." Mr. Prennsteiner showed Mr. Gruber the Leipzig hymn book, which Master Erk had left at St. Peter's. Mr. Gruber was a bit angry, for it was in a different key and the time had been changed, with only four verses. In fact, it had been greatly changed.

"Marie," Franz Gruber called, "Could you bring me the original of **Silent Night***?" But Marie was a spotless housekeeper, and she had long since destroyed the dusty original manuscript.*

In the quiet of his room, Franz Gruber sat down and wrote the history of the song and all six stanzas. This he sent to Master Erk so that corrections could be made in the next printing. He related also that Father Joseph Mohr had died December 4, 1848, as a worthy vicar. Father Mohr died a poor man, having given everything away all his life, even as he had given away his song. How could he know that his gift would be cherished with increasing popularity throughout the years by Christians the world over?

SILENT NIGHT

Silent night, holy night—
All is calm, all is bright.
Round you, Virgin, mother and child;
Holy infant, so tender and mild,
Sleep in heavenly peace—
Sleep in heavenly peace.

Silent night, holy night,
Son of God, how the light
Radiates love from Thy heavenly face,
At the dawn of redeeming grace,
Jesus, Lord, at Thy birth—
Jesus, Lord at Thy birth!

Silent Night, holy night,
Shepherds view the angels' flight;
Kings e'en follow the guiding star;
"Alleluia!" rings near and far,
"Christ, the Saviour, is born—
"Christ, the Saviour, is born."

Silent night, holy night,
From the sky's golden height
Came salvation to every place,
In revealing the fullness of grace:
Jesus, born as a man—
Jesus, born as a man.

Silent night, holy night,
Pouring forth all the might
Of our Father's love and grace,
As Jesus holds in a brother's embrace
All the nations of man—
All the nations of man.

Silent night, holy night—
Ever our promise bright,
Since the fathers' gray-dawning age,
That the Lord will spare in His rage
Children all over the world—
Children all over the world.

Another well-known carol was written by Phillips Brooks, the founder of Trinity Church in Copley Square in Boston. His ambition had long been to visit the Holy Land. In 1865 this dream came true for him. On Christmas Eve he wandered alone in the fields outside Bethlehem. At that time the scene was probably not changed much from the time of that important event almost two thousand years ago. Caught up in the quiet and peace of the night, he wrote **O Little Town of Bethlehem**, *which is one of the best-loved American carols. Often as we sing, we overlook the true beauty of the words, especially since so often only the first verse is sung. But it takes the five verses to receive the full message he intended.*

O LITTLE TOWN OF BETHLEHEM

O little town of Bethlehem
How still we see thee lie!
Above thy deep and dreamless sleep
The silent stars go by.
Yet in thy dark streets shineth
The everlasting light;
The hopes and fears of all the years
Are met in thee to-night.

For Christ is born of Mary;
And gathered all above,
While mortals sleep, the angels keep
Their watch of wond'ring love.
O morning stars, together
Proclaim the holy birth,
And praises sing to God the King,
And peace to men on earth.

How silently, how silently,
The wondrous gift is given!
So God imparts to human hearts
The blessings of His heaven.
No ear may hear his coming,
But in this world of sin,
Where meek souls will receive him still
The dear Christ enters in.

Where children pure and happy
Pray to the blessed Child,
Where misery cries out to thee,
Son of the mother mild;
Where charity stands watching
And faith holds wide the door,
The dark night wakes, the glory breaks,
And Christmas comes once more.

O holy Child of Bethlehem,
Descend to us, we pray;
Cast out our sin, and enter in,
Be born in us today.
We hear the Christmas angels,
The great glad tidings tell:
O come to us, abide with us,
Our Lord Emmanuel.

Thus do carols recall the wonder and meaning of that important night of Christ's birth.

Christmas Appointment

Mazie slammed the phone back on its cradle. "That does it! Everyone has backed out but Rick, Gary, and Christine. We had such a big gang lined up to go caroling," Mazie moaned.

"Then make it a quartet," her mother suggested. "And be grateful that Rick is old enough to drive—thank goodness he's a careful driver, too." Mrs. Matson pulled the curtain aside. "The snow is so deep—the street does look dangerous." She shook her head.

"Do you really think we should go, Mother?" Mazie asked.

"Talk to your father. He's working on his sermon for tonight's Candlelight Service, but this is important, too." Mrs. Matson's frown formed deep lines between her eyebrows.

Mazie tapped on the study door. "Come in," Reverend Matson peered over the top of his glasses at his attractive, long-haired daughter.

"Dad, remember you announced Sunday in services that our youth group would be caroling tonight? All but three 'old faithfuls' have backed out, because of the storm and—they say they're too busy."

"Hmmmm, typical," he mused, absently scanning his notes.

"It isn't worth it for just four of us to go. We'd feel silly and self-conscious. After all, we're hardly that good! Do you suppose those old people will really mind if we don't get to them? I've made all the cookies and candy, but they'd still be good tomorrow. I could take them alone. Why are the kids so indifferent?"

"Mazie, perhaps they don't realize how much those senior church members count on your carols each year. For some of the housebound, this is the only touch of Christmas they have." He paused. "I remember..." and there was a faraway look in his eyes, "I remember a Christmas, before you were born. I had a church post in Maine. Christmas Eve a storm blew in like nothing we'd ever seen. The parsonage was about a block from the church. 'Surely no one would venture out in such a storm,' I said to your mother. She agreed. So we decided it was useless to hold the eleven o'clock Candlelight Service at the church. We called as many people as we could, but the telephone lines were down in most of the town. So we felt completely justified in staying at home toasting our shins by the fire."

"Sounds cozy." Mazie hugged herself before their fire in the grate.

"It was—until a little past eleven, when the doorbell rang. There stood one of the parishioners covered with snow. He said, 'Reverend Matson, are you ill? There must be a hundred people waiting for the service, but the church is locked!"

"How awful! What did you do, Dad?"

"You can believe it didn't take long to get our wraps and boots on. We slipped and slid through the snow on foot to let those faithful people in. I resolved that night never to cancel my responsibilities because of my own discomfort. If even one soul comes, he deserves to be fed."

"Guess you're right—even if there are only four of us—maybe it's the spirit that counts."

"You can be sure you'll brighten some dark homes. Of course, you'll receive more than you give."

At that moment Mrs. Matson entered the room. "Here, Mazie, you've earned the right to wear this cameo. It was given to me that Christmas Eve your father has told you about. It always reminds me to serve faithfully even when the going is rough." She clipped the cameo on the lacy neckband of Mazie's white blouse.

Mazie was the last of the faithful four to be picked up. The four teens were bundled to their eyeballs and snugly booted. "Man, it's slick," Rick laughed as he tucked Mazie into the front seat and slid around to his own door. "We're four goofs, to be sure. What a storm."

"If we visit only Mr. Erickson, it would be worth the effort," Mazie said.

"Nor wind nor hail nor sleet—the postmen and us!" Christine quirped.

First they stopped at blind Mrs. O'Riley's home. She opened her door a crack. "And who may it be on a night like this?" she called out.

The four didn't wait for a deep breath, but started to sing:

"Oh, Come all ye faithful,
Joyful and triumphant..."

"Praises be! Faith and I thought ye'd never venture out tonight. Come in, come in and warm yerselves while ye sing." She threw her door wide as they stamped the snow from their boots and entered the cheery warmth of Mrs. O'Riley's old-fashioned living room. The flames from the fireplace furnished the only light. "Sure'n I don't need a light, but let me turn on the lamp fer ye. Now, sing on! Ye'll never know how I been wishin' fer ye."

The four sang with all the exuberance of youth, and if a voice cracked, it didn't matter. "Like the angels—all o' ye!" Mrs. O'Riley wiped a tear from her eye. "Sure'n those first angels couldn't have sounded any better."

From house to house they drove in the blinding snow. "Well, we've visited everyone but Mr. Erickson. The storm seems to get worse, but we can't by-pass him." Gary was shouting above the howling wind and the noise of the motor.

At Mr. Erickson's small home the four young people spilled out of the car. They broke a path up the drifted walk, shielding their faces from the snow. As they stamped their feet on the porch, the door opened wide. Mr. Erickson was leaning on his cane, his lined face a-glow. The voice was shaky. "Come in, come in. I was afraid the storm would keep you all home and I'd have no Christmas callers this year. Gets a mite lonely around here. Come in by the kitchen stove. As soon as you catch your breath, I'd be much obliged to hear my favorite carols."

Mazie handed Mr. Erickson a box. "Here's some cookies and candy for your Christmas."

"I'll ration them carefully to prolong the pleasure. Bless you!" He patted her hand.

The young quartet loosened their wraps and raised their voices in harmony. Mr. Erickson sat with one gnarled hand clasped over the other on the head of his cane. As they finished *O Little Town of Bethlehem*, he smiled and his eyes grew misty.

"You take me back through the years to Christmases past, filled with family and friends. I've been alone a good many years now—but sing on!" he motioned. Tears streamed down his leathery face as they finished the last strain of

"Away in a manger, no crib for His bed,
The little Lord Jesus lay down His sweet head.
...Asleep the Lord of all."

"We had a son born on Christmas Eve. He was the joy of our lives; but he was so perfect he couldn't stay on earth very long either. Christmas is a time for family reunions, don't you know? Maybe my family reunion isn't far off—"

"Now, now, Mr. Erickson, you mustn't talk like that," Mazie said.

"Why not, young lady. 'Twould be the happiest Christmas of all."

Mazie put her arm around the old shoulders and pressed her young cheek against his wrinkled one. "As long as I can remember I've loved sitting at your feet listening to your stories. How about one now?" He was staring at her throat.

"That cameo," he faltered. "Let me get a good look at it."

She unclasped it and put it in his hand. He examined it and chuckled. "I'd almost forgotten this cameo. You sit down here, Girl—by my rocker." She slipped to the floor and his arthritic hand patted her shiny hair. He leaned back in his chair. "Hmmmm, yes, I remember a Christmas—your coming tonight reminds me of it." He passed the box of cookies and each took one. "It was a night like this—the snow was blowing hard. Most everyone stayed indoors that night. But I couldn't miss Candlelight Service—hadn't missed one in all my life. I lived up in Maine at the time. When I got to the church, it was locked. You'd be surprised how many faithful souls had come out on that terrible night to worship. I walked on to the parsonage, thinking our young minister must surely be sick. I thought nothing could keep him from doing his duty on Christmas Eve. Well, that was a mighty embarrassed young preacher who answered the door." Mr. Erickson chuckled, remembering. "He and his Mrs. made mighty quick time getting to the church to hold that service."

Mazie's eyes mirrored her amazement. "You mean, you were in Dad's parish even then?"

"Sure was. I gave this cameo to your mother. It was my wife's. 'Spect they learned their lesson well, for it's carried on to your generation. You came, too, to keep your appointment tonight."

Rick got to his feet. "I hate to break this up, but it's getting late and we should get home before we're snowbound," he laughed.

As the last gift was opened Christmas morning, Mazie leaned back in her chair with a contented sigh. Then she bolted upright. "Oh, Mother, the cameo you let me wear last night."

"Where is it, Mazie? You didn't lose it, did you?"

"No. Mr. Erickson wanted to examine it. He told me about it. I forgot to get it back."

"Come on, Mazie," her father said. "That cameo will always remind you to be dependable. I'd like to spend a little while with Mr. Erickson anyhow. He'll be lonely, you know."

Mazie breathed deeply as she and her father trudged through the heavy snow to Mr. Erickson's house. Rev. Matson tapped on the door. No answer. He tried the door. It was unlocked.

"Anybody home?" he called. No answer. Mazie grasped her father's hand as they walked into the cold kitchen. She caught her breath, "He hasn't moved since we left last night. My cameo is still on the table where he set it down."

"He—he's gone," her father said.

Mazie smiled through tears. "In his own words, he's had his happiest Christmas, Dad. And we helped to make it so by keeping our Christmas appointment."

What About Angels?

The Old Testament often refers to angels who delivered messages from God or who came to help mortals. So it is not surprising when the New Testament records in Luke that an angel came to the priest Zacharias in the temple. He informed him that his wife Elizabeth would bear a child, who would prepare the way before the Son of God. Then Luke wrote of an angel appearing to Mary and telling her that she was to be the favored one in Israel, who would be the mother of the Savior.

Throughout the scriptures, the people of Israel received messages from on high which were delivered by angels. Therefore, when the Savior was born into the world, the shepherds believed the angel who came and told them of the holy birth. For them to see a multitude of angels singing and praising God was awesome, but not unbelievable.

The Crippled Angel

In the dark wings of the stage, Debbie sat as still as a Christmas mouse, hoping the teachers would never know she was still there. She hoped no one would rush by her and trip over her white ankle-to-thigh cast or her crutch. That morning she had told her mother she must stay for the try-outs for the Christmas pageant. "I'll stay in the wings until you come," she had promised. She had never had enough courage to try in other years. But this year her voice had improved so much that she knew she would be an asset to the chorus, and this would be her last year in elementary school. It was now or never. The Christmas program was always the best program of the whole year, but she had lacked the courage to push herself forward to try for a part. Oh, how she wanted to sing this year.

She looked at her big, ugly cast and sighed. Why did everything have to happen at the wrong time—or was there ever a right time to break a leg?

She was stirred out of her own feeling-sorry-for-herself thoughts by a teacher's voice. "I see no reason why we should even bother with Debbie. Did you ever hear of an angel with cast and crutches?"

"She has such a lovely voice and I half promised her she could be in the production this year," Mrs. Elliott interrupted. "This has been a life-long wish for her. But she's been self-conscious other years to come and try out."

"That was before she broke her leg," Miss Kane replied. "It's out of the question. Angels can't hobble in."

Debbie's ears burned and tears rushed to her eyes. She knew she was going to sniff. Then they would know she was there. That would never do. So she let her nose drip until she could find her hanky. She needed another hand. It was so awkward, hanging onto that crutch so it wouldn't slip and make a noise.

Mrs. Elliott went on. "Couldn't we let her be Mary? We could have her already seated before curtain time and the robes would hide her cast."

"You have to be kidding," Miss Kane argued. "With that mop of red hair and all those freckles, how could she be Mary?"

Mrs. Elliott was silent, thinking. Then she said, "Come on into my room and we'll go over the list again." With a heavy heart, Debbie listened to the echo of the teachers' footsteps on down the hall. On top of being homely, she couldn't do anything right, she moped—couldn't even be an angel in the chorus.

She heard her mother's quick footsteps hurrying down the aisle of the auditorium. "Debbie?" she spoke.

"Up here, Mother," Debbie choked back a sob. Mother mustn't know. She brushed away the tears on her sleeve and put on a smile.

Next day Debbie was surprised but delighted when Mrs. Elliott told her she could be an angel, *if* she could be on stage before anyone else got there. During the days of preparation, she didn't miss a single rehearsal. She had memorized every moment of the pageant. But she must be in position so she wouldn't slow anyone down or be in the way.

Performance night Debbie cautiously made her way through the auditorium and up the dark stage steps behind the heavy, velvet curtain. Her chair was in place. Suddenly it dawned on her that it wasn't right to have an angel on stage in the beginning. The angels had come *after* the birth of Jesus. Why hadn't Mrs. Elliott thought of that? She'd been foolish. Why had she been stubborn and stayed? She struggled with her long, white costume so she wouldn't trip over it on the stairs. As she dragged herself to the top step, she looked up at the star, hanging from the cyclorama. "I'm glad you've given them so much trouble. It keeps them from thinking too much of the trouble I've given them. You're always falling down or won't stay lighted. At least I have company when it comes to doing wrong things." The tears welled up in her eyes, ran down her cheeks and dropped on her white drape. The whole thing was wrong. She wished she was in her usual seat, in the auditorium on the other side of the curtain.

She sat patiently in her chair and waited in the hustle and bustle of the others as they prepared to take their places. Mrs. Elliott draped her leg in a sheet so it would blend with her costume. She patted Debbie on the shoulder, gave her a quick smile, and was on to the next character.

Mary and Joseph entered the stage from the opposite wing and took their places beside the baby doll in the manger. The dim overhead lights gave them an unearthly appearance. Debbie was watching with rapt attention. The wise men took their places. Debbie marveled at their rich robes and jeweled turbans. They stood at their posts with serious faces, caught up in the spirit of the scene. Shepherds took their places.

It was almost time for the curtains to part when the last shepherd hurried from the wing on Debbie's side. He was intent on straightening his long robe under the sash as he hurried to his place, and wasn't watching carefully. Suddenly, he ran straight into Debbie's outstretched broken leg! "Oh!" Debbie gasped and winced with sudden pain. The shepherd was thrown off balance and stumbled, landing in the center of the scene, upsetting the manger, baby and all.

Miss Kane and Mrs. Elliott were suddenly there picking up, straightening, and shushing. Debbie curled up inside. What had she done now, just by being there? If she could only disappear. She was certainly a jinx.

Miss Kane held up the end of an extension cord and said in a whisper to Mrs. Elliott, "Wouldn't you know? Now the star is disconnected. We'll never get it to work right. A wonder it didn't come crashing down. I could say 'I told you so.' It's all her fault." And she shot an angry glance in Debbie's direction.

The lump in Debbie's throat was choking her, but she mustn't give way to tears—not here. Miss Kane jammed the extension into the outlet and connected the star. "Please light, star, at the right time—" Debbie breathed, "and don't fall. Please, please." Instantly the scene was righted. A hush fell on the stage as the curtain parted. The star did come on and shed its white light on the Nativity scene. The pianist quietly began to play the introduction to the angels' singing. Debbie glanced toward the black curtain which hid the angels. It should be open by now. Mrs. Elliott, the musical director, was seated in front of the stage, poised to bring the angels in at the right instant. The black curtain didn't move. A frantic look crossed Mrs. Elliott's face, and she stared straight at Debbie with a don't-let-me-down-now expression. Would the angels behind the black curtain know enough to start singing? They didn't. On the downbeat, Debbie sang out over the lump in her throat, "Silent night, Holy night!"

"Keep singing!" Mrs. Elliott's lips mouthed the words to Debbie.

"All is calm, all is bright—" she continued in a clear, sweet voice. By the time she had reached "Christ the Savior is born," the black curtain was open, revealing a chorus of angels. Sensing Mrs. Elliott's wishes, they all started the second verse and went on to the third, finishing with a glorious "*Christ the Savior is born!*"

When the performance came to a reverent close, audience and cast were caught in its spell. Mrs. Elliott hurried to Debbie's chair and hugged her tightly. "Bless you, Debbie. If you hadn't been out in front, the whole thing would have been ruined. You—leg, cast, and all—saved the show!"

The lump was there again, but this time there were tears of joy.

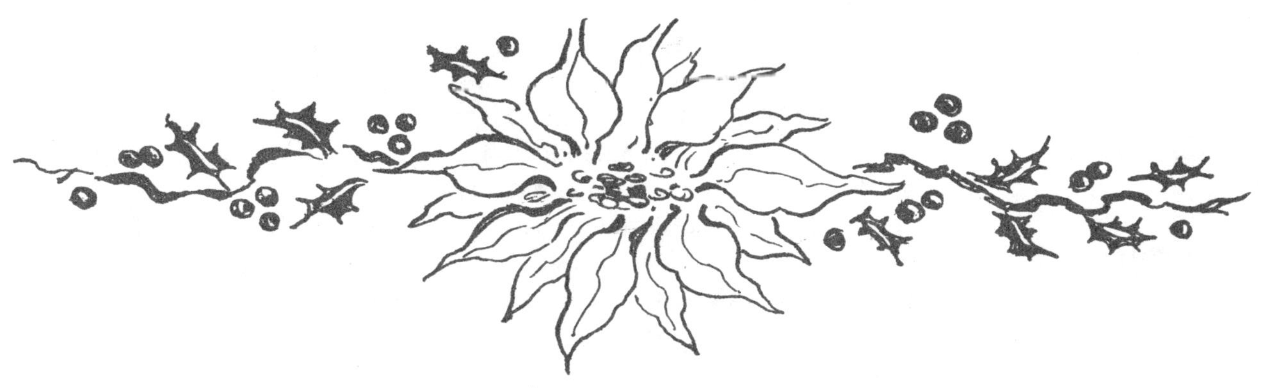

The Angel's Voice

Wisps of clouds, drifting through the sky, blotted out the twinkling stars. The angel choir grouped together on a billowing cloudbank in heaven.

Angel Eli, the conductor, tapped his baton on his music stand and scowled at the tousle-haired angel on the front row. He scolded, "Joshua, you're our boy soprano. Why didn't you come in on your obligato?"

Joshua's mouth opened wide and he pointed to his throat. "Nothing comes out," he said, but only his lips moved.

"Eh?" Eli cupped his hand around his ear and leaned forward, the better to hear.

"Nothing comes out," Joshua whispered. "I've lost my voice."

"Lost your voice, did you say? Well, you'd better find it. For ages we've practiced for our big night. The birth of the Christ Child is close. Hmmm," Eli frowned, wrinkling his brow. "There's no time to waste. We'll find a replacement for you."

"Oh, no, please don't!" Tears filled Joshua's eyes. "Please, please let me sing." But no one heard his words.

"We need you, Joshua, but how can you sing if you've lost your voice?" Eli roared. "Now who could sing that obligato? Hmmm—let's see—there's David—He has the voice if he would sing. But he's such a sad angel. We need joyful singers to announce the birth of the Holy Child. David has never practiced with us. Well, let's sing." Eli's face brightened. "This is to be the most glorious chorus ever to be heard on earth—or in heaven, for that matter. The Savior's birth is the greatest event in history." Then he looked down at Joshua and scowled again. "Joshua, if you don't find your voice quickly, we'll have to replace you." He raised his eyes to the group. "All right, let's try it again—without Joshua." He tapped his baton and raised his arms. The rolling tones of the harps played the introduction, and the chorus came in on the downbeat: "Glory to God in the highest," they sang.

Joshua listened. It wasn't the same without that high obligato. His heart felt as if it would break. With downcast eyes, he slipped from his place on the front row, back through all the flowing white robes of the vast chorus. Through long ages Joshua had counted on singing that soprano obligato. There was nothing he loved to do so much as to sing. But where could he find his voice?

He wandered down one golden street after another. At last he approached the pearly gates, where St. Peter stood guard. Joshua ran up to him and touched his hand. St. Peter looked down at the small angel. "Oh, Joshua, you startled me—sneaking up on me without your usual singing."

"I've lost my voice," Joshua said, but the words didn't come out.

"Lost your voice?" St. Peter was aghast. "That's serious. How can you sing the obligato with the choir if you've lost your voice?"

"Where can I find my voice?" Joshua whispered in St. Peter's ear.

"My, my, how would I know where to find your voice? I didn't lose it." He thought and he thought. "I believe you're looking for something you can't really find. It's still inside you. You must find the way to get it out. Did you try standing on your head? Maybe your voice slipped down inside."

Joshua stood on his head. Oh, that was embarrassing. Whoever saw an angel in a position like that? St. Peter politely turned his back and waited. Joshua waved his legs, trying to jolt his voice back into his throat. He bounced back on his feet and his gown fell back into place. He opened his mouth and tried to sing, but nothing came out. St. Peter shook his head and shrugged his shoulders.

Joshua walked on through more golden streets. Next he saw an Angel of the Peace who was making his rounds of the heavenly city. Joshua slipped up behind him and touched his golden billy-club. "Please, sir, could you tell me where I could find my voice?"

The Angel of the Peace looked down at him in surprise. "It can't be you, Joshua, without a song on your lips!"

"I've lost my voice." But nothing came out.

The Angel of the Peace put his ear to Joshua's mouth and Joshua whispered. The angel tapped rhythmically on his golden billy-club with his fingertips. It was the rhythm of *Glory to God in the Highest*, and Joshua felt he would burst with wanting to sing it. "I'm the star. They can't sing it without my obligato." But the words couldn't be heard. The Angel of the Peace hummed and hawed for a few moments and then his face lighted up with an idea.

"Joshua, why don't you go to the Angel of the Apothecary. He might know how to cure you."

That was a wonderful idea, and Joshua ran off down the golden street toward the apothecary. He opened the door and hurried in. The bell above the door tinkled and the Angel of the Apothecary came from the back room.

"Oh, it's you, Joshua. You're not singing. I heard only the bell."

"I've lost my voice." Only his lips moved and the words didn't come out. But the Angel of the Apothecary could read lips, so it didn't matter.

"How can I get it back—do you know?" Joshua whispered.

"Well, let me see." He went into the back room and looked at all the labels on his bottles. Then he came back with a clear fluid in a small bottle. "Here, Joshua. Try this. It's distilled heavenly dew. Take a sip and gargle and then swallow it."

Joshua obeyed. Then he opened his mouth and expected music to break forth, but nothing happened. The Angel of the Apothecary shrugged his shoulders and said, "That's the only suggestion I have."

The tears rolled down Joshua's cheeks and his shoulders sagged. He wandered down another golden street. As he turned the corner, whom should he meet but David. David's face was sad, as usual. It made Joshua even sadder to look at him.

"Hi, David," Joshua greeted, but the words couldn't be heard.

David looked puzzled. "What's the matter, Joshua?"

"I've lost my voice. Oh, David, if I can't find my voice, I can't sing in the choir and you know the greatest event in history is almost here. Eli is very angry with me."

"I'm sorry. Truly I am, Joshua. I know how much you like to sing. I like to sing, too, but there's no chance for any other boy soprano with you around."

"David, the chorus is more important than any one person." Joshua suddenly had an idea. "If I teach you my part, will you sing it? For once in your life, could you be joyful?"

David's face lighted up. "Oh, Joshua, for ages I've wanted to sing in the choir. Something inside me needs to sing. It makes me sad when it doesn't come out. If you'll teach me the part, I'll be the happiest angel in all of heaven. I'll sing with all my heart."

Joshua pulled out his choir book and his pitchpipe from the big pocket in his robe. Line by line Joshua taught David the music. David was bursting with happiness. Before long he knew every note he was to sing.

Next day Joshua took David by the hand and led him down the street to the clouds where the heavenly choir was practicing. Eli scowled down at Joshua. "Did you find your voice, young angel?"

Joshua shook his head sadly. He whispered in Eli's ear, "I taught David my part and he's ready to sing it."

Eli turned to David, expecting the usual sad look. But instead David was smiling proudly. Eli smiled back and said, "Take your place on the front row, Angel David." Then Eli turned to the whole group and announced: "Tonight is the great night we've all been waiting for. God will send His Son to earth to teach men how to live. He will give His life to save mankind. He will teach men: 'He that loseth his life shall find it.' Come, let us practice. Lose yourselves in the music and you will find new life." He raised his baton and the harp tones rolled forth. The chorus came in on the downbeat. Joshua's heart was in his throat. He wanted to sing so much, it almost choked him. He listened closely as David sang the obligato. David didn't miss a note. It was heavenly. When they were through, Joshua clapped his hands and shouted in a loud voice, "Bravo! Bravo!"

"Joshua!" Eli cried. "You've found your voice! You will sing with us."

David looked at Joshua, and tears welled up in his eyes. "Then you won't be needing me," he said softly and slipped out of his place to make room for Joshua.

"No, no, David," Joshua held him back. "Eli, could David sing with me?"

"Of course," Eli smiled.

A bright light enveloped the angels. "The star!" Eli shouted. All eyes turned toward earth. In the rays of a blinding star, a humble stable was outlined. The angels moved toward the earth to a group of shepherds watching their flocks. Eli gave the downbeat and the sound of the heavenly choir filled the clear night air. Never had there been such a night, and never had there been such a chorus! Joshua squeezed David's hand and winked at him. Joshua's heart was pounding. In finding David's voice, I found my own, he thought. It is as the Christ will teach mankind: Whosoever shall lose his life for my sake, shall find it!

What About
Stars?

Astronomers have never solved the mystery of the Star of Bethlehem. However, four theories have been proposed as explanations.

The first theory is that a very great meteor appeared. But the light of a meteor lasts only a few seconds and would be seen only in a certain locality.

The second theory is that a comet appeared in the eastern sky. Comets last for days and have been so bright they could be seen even in daylight. They move slowly and can be seen from night to night. The Chinese recorded such a comet in the year 4 B.C. and it appeared in the spring of the year, February to April. But this was not a star.

The third theory is that of a new star. Tradition says that Hipparchus[1] *noted a brilliant new star in 134 B.C. where no star had been seen before. He was so surprised by this sight that he charted the visible stars in the heavens. Since then a number of new stars have appeared at intervals, but they have been only temporary stars, and faded away again.*

The fourth theory is the coming together of two or more of the planets. Those that can be seen with the naked eye are Saturn, Jupiter, Mars, and Venus. If any three of these should come together, it would be remarkable. In 706 B.C. it was recorded that Jupiter, Saturn, and Mars seemed to come together. Several times since, this has happened.

Hopi Indian legends, handed down from the ancients, tell of the brilliant new star which appeared on the American continent to their forefathers and informed them of the birth of their White Brother across the waters.

Matthew recorded in the Bible that the star guided the Wise Men to the Savior. In the **Book of Mormon** *(3 Nephi 1) we read of a "bright, new star" which was seen on the American continent. Because of prophecies that had been recorded, the people knew this marked the Savior's birth across the sea.*

Even though we do not know the origin of this great star, we do know that it existed. Many people saw it and the records have come down through the ages to us. Because it was seen at the time of the Savior's birth, stars have become an important symbol of the Christmas season.

---

[1] Pronounced Hy-PAR-kuhs

The Star in the New World

At last the carving is finished," exclaimed Zeniff as he smiled down at his lame brother who had waited patiently in the cart. "I will carry you inside so you can see for yourself." Zeniff lifted Shim in his strong arms and carried him up the steps of the temple. Shim sat in front of the carving admiring the workmanship, as Zeniff picked up a sheepskin and wiped the dust carefully out of each carved nook, rubbing and polishing.

"It is perfect," Shim smiled. "Do you think the Savior will really look like that when He comes some day to teach us?"

"Perhaps," the Chief Judge nodded. "You have done well, Zeniff, to complete your father's work. When he returns to Zarahemla, I shall settle with him. There is so much wickedness among the people, perhaps this will strengthen the faith of those who see it. If your father can find the right stone, other carvings similar to this may do much good. But I am almost afraid to display it. It is difficult to know the believers from the unbelievers, and this may bring persecution upon your father."

"I hope not," Zeniff sighed.

"Zeniff, you must get your lame brother home. I do not like what I hear on the streets this day. I wish your father were here—you may need him."

"I wish he were here, too," Zeniff agreed.

With a wave of his hand, the Chief Judge dismissed Zeniff. The tall boy tucked Shim in the cart, then picked up the tongue of the cart and pulled it through the streets. On the outskirts of Zarahemla, Zeniff sat on a large rock by the road. "I must rest," he puffed. "You are getting heavy, little brother."

"Oh, Zeniff, thank you for taking me to see the carving. But tell me, what worries the Chief Judge?" Shim lifted his withered legs to a more comfortable position in the small cart.

"You are inside so much, you do not hear the street talk." Suddenly Zeniff put his finger to his lips and looked anxiously toward two men, approaching. One spoke in an excited voice, gesturing with his hands.

"I tell you, we have been patient too long. They do not deserve to live, those foolish ones who believe that the signs Samuel foretold will still come to pass."

His companion nodded. "Tonight is the night of destruction."

Zeniff recognized the dark man. He had seen him in the temple. Was he an unbeliever? The Chief Judge was right. You couldn't tell the difference. Suddenly the dark man noticed Zeniff and Shim. He jerked his head in their direction and sneered, "Ha, are not these the sons of the sculptor?"

The other agreed. "I've heard their father is away, searching for some special stone. In the temple I saw his carving. He'll never live to carve more, nor will his sons. Their God has forsaken them and their prophets speak falsehoods. The time is past for the signs of their Savior's coming. Who will deliver them when their destruction begins—tonight?" He threw back his head and laughed loudly.

As soon as the men had walked on, Shim asked, "What do they mean?"

"Just what they say, little brother. Even I am no longer sure of what I believe. Perhaps they are right—the time is past for the appearance of the signs of the Savior's birth. Samuel said, in five years we would have a day and a night and a day of light, and then a bright new star would appear in the heavens. Then we would know the Savior is born in the land where our forefathers came from."

"When our mother lived, she told us how she heard Samuel prophesying from the city walls," Shim said. "Zeniff, you must not lose your faith. The signs will come. My brother, all things are possible, if we believe. God will take care of us."

Zeniff's face suddenly became clouded and angry. "How can you say that? You, who have been crippled from birth! Have we not prayed all your life that you would be made whole? God has not heard our prayers. Perhaps the unbelievers are right and we are wrong."

Shocked, Shim sat in silence.

Zeniff jerked the cart as he started. Neither boy spoke the rest of the way. At home Zeniff lifted Shim to the bed, then left him, for it was long past time for the evening meal. Worried, Shim picked up a lump of clay on the bedside table and began to push here and squeeze there with his skillful fingers. "It will soon be dark," Shim said to himself, "and Zeniff will feel better in the morning. But perhaps Zeniff thinks morning might never come for us. If only Father would return, he would know what to do. Of course—that was why Zeniff was sharp. He didn't know what to do with me. Zeniff could run and hide from the unbelievers, but he couldn't carry me very far, so he must stay and face destruction with a cripple." What could they do?

At last Zeniff came with food, two meal cakes and dried dates. "I have been working so hard on Father's carving, I hadn't noticed how low our food is getting," Zeniff apologized. Shim noticed that Zeniff's eyes were red. He bit into his meal cake.

"Is Zeniff thinking we won't need any more food because they will come tonight?" Shim pondered.

Zeniff noticed the piece of clay Shim had almost finished molding—a babe wrapped in swaddling clothes.

"It's very good," Zeniff said, examining the detail. "What a shame you will never be able to stand and carve like Father."

"Some day I will stand even as you do. When my faith is strong enough, my legs will be strong also."

"Is this why you have molded a babe?" Zeniff asked.

"It gives me strength inside. The Savior will soon come to the earth as a babe, as the prophets have foretold. And some day, after his work across the water is finished, he will come here. We will see him and know him." He paused.

"Zeniff, have you noticed that the sun has set in the west, and yet it is still light?"

Zeniff stared out the doorway. "You are right. Hmmm, strange—" Suddenly distant noises caught their attention. Angry voices were coming nearer. Children cried. A woman screamed. Shim saw Zeniff's face turn white. "Where can we hide?" Zeniff cried.

"There is no place to hide," Shim said calmly. "Only God can help us, Zeniff."

The storm of angry noises was outside now and Shim heard a loud voice shout, "Does not the sculptor live here?"

The dark man almost filled the doorway, his face evil. He moved to the bed and towered over Shim, gloating over his helplessness. The dark man noticed the clay carving on the table. Picking it up, he mashed it in his big hand and slammed it to the floor. "I see you believe also," he sneered. "And who will protect you now?"

"It is not dark outside yet," Shim said.

"You have no place to hide," the man swaggered about the room.

"Yet the sun went down long ago," Shim said. "Why is it not dark?" The man looked at him sharply and then stared outside. Shim continued, "It is the sign—the sign Samuel foretold—and there shall be a day and a night and a day of light." The dark man looked as if he had been hit from behind with a club. He stumbled out of the house to his companions who were milling around outside.

"The boy's right," he shouted. "The sun has set, but it's still as light as mid-day." Silence settled on the throng. From the bed, Shim watched the men as they mumbled to each other and, like slinking dogs, they went their separate ways.

Zeniff dropped to his knees by the bed, burying his face in his hands. "I am weak, Shim. Your legs are withered, but you are stronger than I."

The night passed in wonder and it remained as mid-day. Next morning the sun rose and the day drew on. "If only Father would come," Zeniff said. "I'm uneasy—such strange happenings. I don't know what to expect next. Shim, it is the time of the Savior's birth."

"Do you think he looks like this?" Shim held up a second model of a babe in swaddling clothes. "Darkness falls outside and yet I am not tired—no rest for these two days and a night and yet I am not weary."

Hearing hurried footsteps, Zeniff stepped to the door. "Father—it is Father, Shim," Zeniff exclaimed.

"Oh, my sons, I have been deeply concerned for you. The unbelievers did much mischief before they came to know that the light all night was one of the promised signs. Are you unharmed?"

"We are safe, Father," Shim smiled. Suddenly he pointed toward the doorway. "Father! Zeniff! Do you see the light in the sky? See! At last it is the promised star!" Shim rose from the bed, his eyes fixed to the rays of the brightest star he had ever seen. He walked to the door and spoke softly, "Christ, the Savior, is born."

The father and Zeniff held their breath as they watched Shim walk through the doorway and out into the clear, bright night. Zeniff whispered, "His faith has made him whole."

Bibliography

PERSONAL INTERVIEWS

Miss ElsBritt Bloomquist, 224 South 12th East, Salt Lake City, Utah (A native of Finland, from a section nearest Sweden.)

Mrs. Pauline D. Poulsen, 2608 Sherwood Drive, Salt Lake City, Utah, who lived in Finland.

MAGAZINE ARTICLE

Storer, Doug, "The Flower of Christmas," *Boys' Life*, December, 1967, pp. 26-27.

BOOKS

Adshead, Gladys L., *Brownies—It's Christmas*. Henry Z. Walck, Inc., New York, N. Y. 1955.

Alden, Raymond MacDonald, *Why The Chimes Rang*. Bobbs-Merrill Co., Inc., New York, N. Y. 1954.

Auld, William Muir, *Christmas Traditions*. The MacMillan Co., Inc., New York, N. Y. 1831.

Barnett, James H., *The American Christmas, A Study in National Culture*. The MacMillan Co., Inc., New York, N. Y. 1954.

Bickerstaff, George, *Christmas in Story for L.D.S. Readers*. Bookcraft, Inc., Salt Lake City, Utah 1969.

Book of Mormon. An account written by the hand of Mormon on Plates taken from the Plates of Nephi. Translated by Joseph Smith, Jun. (First English edition, 1830.) Salt Lake City, Utah. Published by The Church of Jesus Christ of Latter-day Saints.

Brandley, Franklyn M., *The Christmas Sky.* Thomas Y. Crowell Company, New York, N. Y. 1966.

Brinkerhoff, Zula C., *God's Chosen People In America.* Salt Lake City, Utah 1971.

Carlson, Natalie Savage, *Befana's Gift.* Harper & Row, Publishers, New York, N. Y. 1969.

Caudill, Rebecca, *A Certain Small Shepherd.* Holt, Rinehart & Winston, New York, N. Y. 1965.

Cavanah, Frances, *Told Under the Christmas Tree.* Grosset & Dunlap, New York, N. Y. 1941.

Christmas in Many Lands, a compilation by L. C. Page & Company, Publishers, Boston, Mass. 1894.

Count, Earl W., *Four Thousand Years of Christmas.* Henry Schuman, New York, N. Y.

Dawson, W. F., *Christmas, Its Origin and Associations.* Elliot Stock, London 1902.

Dickinson, Asa Don and Skinner, Adam M. (Ed.), *The Children's Book of Christmas Trees.* Doubleday & Co., Inc., New York, N. Y. 1955.

Driver, Olive, *The Christmas Story*. Exposition Press, New York, N. Y. 1951.

Engle, Paul, *Prairie Christmas*. Longmans, Green & Co., New York, N. Y.

Foley, Daniel J., *Christmas in the Good Old Days.* Chilton Co., Book Division, Publishers, Philadelphia and New York, N. Y. 1961.

Foley, Daniel J., *Christmas the World Over.* Chilton Company, Philadelphia and New York, N. Y. 1963.

Foley, Daniel J., *The Christmas Tree.* Chilton Company, Philadelphia and New York, N. Y. 1960.

Gardner, Horace J., *Let's Celebrate Christmas.* A. S. Barnes & Company, New York, N. Y. 1940.

Graham, Eleanor, *Happy Holidays*. E. P. Dutton & Company, Inc., New York, N. Y. 1933.

Hadfield, John, *The Christmas Companion*. E. P. Dutton & Co., Inc., New York, N. Y. 1939.

Hadfield, Miles and John, *The Twelve Days of Christmas.* Little, Brown & Co., Boston, Mass. 1961.

Hansen, L. Taylor, *He Walked the Americas.* Amherst Press, Amherst, Wis. 1963.

Holy Bible, The, Authorized King James Version. Cleveland: World Publishing Company, Luke 2 and Matthew 2.

Hottes, Alfred Carl, *One Thousand and One Christmas Facts and Fancies.* Dodd, Mead & Company, New York, N. Y. 1937.

Ideals Publication, *Christmas Around the World.* Ideals Publishing Company, Milwaukee, Wis. 1961.

Johnson, Lois S., *Christmas Stories 'Round the World.* Rand, McNally & Company, New York, N. Y. 1960.

Krythe, Mamie R., *All About Christmas.* Harper & Bros., New York, N. Y.

Lefevre, Kamiel, *Bells Over Belgium.* Belgian Government Information Center, New York, N. Y. 1949.

Morris, Ernest, *Legends O' The Bells,* Sampson Low, Marston & Co., Ltd., London.

Morton, H. V., *In the Steps of the Master.* Dodd, Mead & Co., New York, N. Y. 1935.

Patterson, Lillie, *Christmas Feasts and Festivals.* Garrard Publishing Co., Champaign, Ill. 1968.

Pauli, Hertha, *Silent Night.* Alfred A. Knopf, New York, N. Y. 1956.

Pauli, Hertha, *St. Nicholas' Travels.* Houghton, Mifflin Co., Boston, Mass. 1945.

Pauli, Hertha, *The First Christmas Tree.* Ives Washburn, Inc., New York, N. Y. 1961.

Sechrist, Elizabeth Hough, *Christmas Everywhere.* Macrae-Smith Company, Philadelphia, Pa. 1936.

Smith, Elva S. and Hazeltine, Alice I., *Christmas in Legend and Story.* Lothrop, Lee & Shepard Company, Boston, Mass. 1915.

Thayne, Mirla Greenwood, *When He Comes Again.* Deseret Book Co., Salt Lake City, Utah.

Then, John N., *Christmas, A Collection of Christmaslore*. The Bruce Publishing Co., Milwaukee, Wis. 1934.

Then, John N., *Christmas Comes Again*. A second book of Christmaslore. The Bruce Publishing Co., Milwaukee, Wis. 1939.

Watts, Franklin, *The Complete Christmas Book*. Edited and published by Franklin Watts, Inc., New York, N. Y. 1958.

Wernecke, Herbert H., *Christmas Songs and Their Stories*. Westminster Press, Philadelphia, Pa.